OUT OF THE ASHES

Finding the Purpose in Your Pain

D'Andre J. Lacy

Out Of The Ashes:

Finding the Purpose in Your Pain

Copyright@2020 D'Andre J. Lacy

ISBN: 979-8-55014-786-3

Author: D'Andre Lacy

Editor: Valerie L. McDowell

Cover Design: Daniel O. Ojedokun

Cover Photography: Shickerra Lacy of Key Kandids

Publisher: Power2Excel

Printed in the United States of America.

ALL RIGHTS RESERVED. This book contains material protected under International and Federal Copyright Laws and Treaties. Any unauthorized reprint or use of this material is prohibited. No part of this book may be reproduced or transmitted in any form or by any means, electronic or mechanical, including photocopying, recording, or by any information storage and retrieval system without express written permission from the author Danlacy18@gmail.com.

Dedication

*I dedicate this book to my beautiful wife, Shickerra.
Your love gave me the courage to write this book.
You give meaning to everything I do.*

*To my mother, DaWanda, your resiliency and strength in
the face of adversity have always inspired me.
Thank you for all of your sacrifices that allowed me to
prosper.*

Foreword

Deeply refreshed.

Isn't that how you want to feel after you finish reading a book or having a heart to heart with a true friend?

The content of the book or conversation may not be light or surface level, but there is something about written or spoken words that can calm the soul and help redirect our feet down the right path.

Only a true faithful man of God with a humble posture could be so bold to take his life's story filled with trials and tribulations and share it with the world. D'Andre, with Christ's power and a servant's heart, has fiercely charged into the unknown to shed light on the darkness of his past and present so you and I may know one thing, To God, "even darkness is not dark to [Him]; the night is bright as the day, for darkness is as light with [Him]" (Psalm 139:12).

Out of the Ashes is not the first time D'Andre has faithfully pursued God's purpose for his life. In the Summer of 2019, on a single day's notice and with a multitude of unknowns, he answered the call to travel and help me lead 10 high schoolers that he had never met before to an Athletes in Action Inner City sports camp in Xenia, Ohio. Never having met D'Andre before the trip myself, we both had no idea of what to expect, but we should have known that God hits moving targets best. When you courageously say yes to what God has in store for you, it allows for the Spirit to work in ways you would have never imagined.

So is this it? Do we close the book now or step into the unknown? Do we hide the real issues that rage war within us, or do we confront them head on and bring them to the light? Beyond this page you will read about very real and raw experiences written in a genuine and conversationalist way that may stir things inside of you. I challenge you to answer these stirrings in a form of action. No longer should our sins and imperfections rule and enslave us. Allow for conversations to be had, grieving when needed, and seek to bring what is kept in the dark into the light because your darkness is not dark to our Savior and King.

To my brother D'Andre, thank you for consistently trusting the Lord and following Him. Your friendship and commitment to others is that of Joshua towards David. Your bravery is cutting a pathway for many to follow. To God be the praise and glory.

-Blake Fox

Former MLB Player, Milwaukee Brewers

All-American at Rice University

Table of Contents

Dedication. 3

Foreword. 5

Introduction. 9

Part I: The Fire

Chapter 1:   You Are Not an Accident 15

Chapter 2:   Embrace Your Origins. 25

Chapter 3:   Remove the Labels 47

Part II: The Ashes

Chapter 4:   Hold On to Your Hope 67

Chapter 5:   Mourn Your Innocence 75

Chapter 6:   Address the Addictions 81

Part III: The Rebirth

Chapter 7:   Take Ownership. 95

Chapter 8:   Challenge the B.S.. 101

Chapter 9:   Live in Your Purpose 115

Conclusion. 127

Introduction

"If I died, would anyone even notice?"

The pain I endured throughout different phases of my life once made me feel hopeless and caused me to question my very existence. I never attempted suicide, but not waking up seemed like a better option than facing the adversity that was awaiting me the next day. However, what happens to us is not as important as how we respond to what happens to us.

"Pain is your friend."- Master Chief John Urgayle I G.I.Jane

Or at least that's what Master Chief John Urgayle says in G.I.Jane. Can pain really be your ally? He says the best part of pain is, "It lets you know you're not dead yet!" I have some fantastic news for you: You have survived ALL of your worst days!

Say this aloud to yourself, "(Your name), you have survived all of your worst days."

What if your pain was not a bad thing? What if I told you that all of the pain you have experienced has counted for something? Imagine the blessing in knowing that everything you've endured was just preparing you for something bigger than yourself? If all of this is true, then what would stop anyone from walking into their destiny?

Several things stop us, and they're usually all painful.

Guilt.

Shame.

Our past.

Childhood trauma.

But it all boils down to perspective.

We can choose to see the scars left by these experiences just as reminders of what hurts us, or we can realize they are also indicators of healing and survival.

Unfortunately, for many of us, when thoughts of our past come to mind, we believe they make us unworthy and unlovable. I, too, faced this same predicament until I realized that the very things that I once hated about myself were actually some of my most appealing qualities. The things that I once thought disqualified me were the very things that qualified me to be used by God for His glory.

When we encounter calamities in life, the tendency is to seek someone out who has had the same experiences as we have. We want to be reassured by someone who has walked a mile in our shoes, not just someone with a bunch of information and advice that they've never had to use themselves. The question is, "How can we expect to find such a person if we all resist and resent the storms of life that come our way?"

"It's not about you!"

That's the opening line of one of the best-selling books of all time: *The Purpose Driven Life*. I agree wholeheartedly with this statement. At the core of all negative emotions is an inward focus. If you're willing to do the work it takes to facilitate your healing process, you'll discover that your pain can be repurposed for the benefit of others.

In her book *iQUIT: The How-To Guide to Letting Go of Everything That Is Holding You Back,* Rachel B-Foy writes, "Someone is waiting for you to operate in your purpose so that they can operate in theirs. Understand that you are: the solution to someone's prayer and the 'permission' someone so desperately awaited." Someone else's freedom is dependent upon you walking fully in your purpose.

But what does walking in your purpose look like?

Walking in your purpose means trusting that what you need to become the person God created you to be is already inside of you. Once you are clear about that, then ask yourself, "What am I passionate about? What are my values? My goals?" Then, start taking action every day to get moving toward those things. And ultimately, you will find yourself living a more fulfilled and more authentic life.

The inspiration for the title of this book comes from one of my favorite promises from God: ..."To appoint unto them that mourn in Zion, to give unto them beauty for ashes, the oil of joy for mourning, the garment of praise for the spirit of heaviness..." (Isaiah 61:3 KJV)

This promise is one that has kept me going through many trials along my journey. So, if you are ready to repurpose your pain and begin the journey of discovering your purpose and walking into your destiny, then this book is for you.

I am excited for your willingness to pursue the higher calling that God has placed on your life from the time you were born. May you be blessed and changed by what you read.

Part I
THE FIRE

The phoenix is a mythical creature with a fascinating life cycle. As it approaches death, it begins to build a nest for itself. Once the nest is complete, it sets itself on fire and is consumed by the flames.

Unlike the phoenix, we didn't get to choose our "nest" at the beginning of our lives. However, we can relate to the fire that consumes this majestic bird. We all have been through some sort of "fire" in our lives.

Chapter 1

YOU ARE NOT AN ACCIDENT

> For I know the plans I have for you," declares the LORD, "plans to prosper you and not to harm you, plans to give you hope and a future.
> Jeremiah 29:11 NIV

I'm a bastard?!

You don't know how much I would love to see the look on some of your faces as you read that question. Many people would consider it a profane thing to say-especially when referring to oneself. *Bastard* has become a tool for the angry to demean the object of their fury, but that is not how the term originated. The meaning of words tends to evolve over time.

The word *bastard* has Latin roots going back to the medieval period. The original term bastard refers to a pack-saddle. Basts were used as makeshift beds during long treks. The ending *ard* was placed on the end to form the term *bastardus* to describe a person who was conceived on one of these temporary beds. In layman's terms, a *bastard is* a person who was born to unmarried parents. Over time, the word began to also be used to describe despicable, disagreeable people.

So the question remains: Do I consider myself a bastard?

No and yes.

Part of maturing as a person is the realization that two things can be true at the same time. I would not say I am a despicable or disagreeable person, but my parents were not married when I was conceived. By definition--you guessed it-- that makes me a bastard, aka a love child. I love my parents (and they did get married later), but I'm going to go out on a limb here and say that I was not a part of their plans at the time.

When you're young, you tend to see life through rose-colored glasses. I knew I was born prior to their marriage, but it took a while for me to process what that truly meant. When it finally hit me that I was unplanned and unexpected, I often wondered several things:

Did I ruin my parents' lives?

Do they resent having me?

How much of a role did my birth play in them getting married?

How different would their lives have been had I not been born?

Eventually, these questions culminated into one thought:

Am I an accident?

I don't think I'm alone in questioning my existence. In a day and age that has some of the highest rates of suicide, depression and anxiety in history, I know others are wrestling with wondering what their purpose in life truly is. Before we can even consider delving into the question of why we were born and what we were placed on this earth to do, we must first come to grips with the issue of whether or not we should have been born in the first place.

Maybe you have a story similar to mine - or perhaps yours is much more detrimental to your wellbeing. I do not believe in the notion of competing over whose childhood trauma was the worst, but I acknowledge that there is someone, somewhere who would trade their upbringing for mine any day of the week. Life is not so much about what happens to you, but rather it's more about your perspective and response to what has happened.

How did you enter this world? Were you a "love child" like me? The product of a broken home? Were you put up for adoption? Abandoned as an infant? Maybe you were born to a single parent and never met your mother or father. If any of these scenarios reflect your life story or apply to you directly in some way, then I have five words for you:

You are **NOT** an accident!

As a follower of Jesus Christ and a Bible-believer, I see life through a biblical worldview. I experience peace and comfort by meditating on and applying the principles found in God's Word so I can watch his promises manifest in my life. One truth that is consistently spoken throughout the Bible is the understanding that our words have power.

Proverbs 18:21 (NIV) says, "The tongue has the power of life and death, and those who love it will eat its fruit." Throughout this book, I will ask you to speak affirmations to yourself out loud. I believe we often give our doubts, fears, and insecurities the upper hand, causing us to then become prisoners of our own mind.

In any team sport, the concept of a home court advantage is frequently mentioned - especially in really important games. It is generally believed that the home team has a mental edge over their opponent. Not only is there comfort in playing in an arena or stadium or on a field that is familiar to the home team, they also have the support of thousands of fans cheering them on.

The team that is playing on their home court can feed off of the energy of the hometown crowd, and the sheer volume of the fans has the potential to disrupt the communication of the visiting team. It can be so loud that you can't even hear your own thoughts over the noise of the opposing team's fans.

Our enemy, Satan, has a "home court advantage" in the confines of your mind. If your house were on fire, would you grab a flamethrower to extinguish the flames? No! Now I know that conventional wisdom says we should think positive thoughts, but if the problem started in your mind, that is not where you will experience victory. With that said, I need you to say the following:

"I am **not** an accident! I was created by God!"

I want you to feel free to say this as many times as you need to say it. If you don't have a daily affirmation routine, I strongly encourage that you start one. Personify your negative thoughts and speak directly to them. Name your negative thoughts "Tyrone" (or whatever name you'd like) and tell Tyrone where he can go! At first, you may need to repeat these words many times throughout the day, but eventually they will begin to take root in your spirit, and you will believe what you are saying about yourself.

I already know what some of you are thinking: "Cool story bro, but you don't understand just how messed up the start of my life was." You may really believe that you were someone's mistake or maybe someone literally said the words "You are a mistake" or "I didn't want you!" There are situations in which people are so stressed by the pressures of parenthood that they transfer those negative emotions to their children and cause them to feel like a burden. Any child who thinks they are resented for just being alive would naturally question their value. **One of the reasons our parents have the potential to hurt us so badly is because we give them too much credit, and don't give God enough!**

Remember, two things can be true concurrently. It is not my intention to refute any part of your life experiences. What I do desire is to challenge you to add another dimension to your perspective concerning those same situations. It may be true that your family didn't plan for your arrival, but it is also true that God "knitted [you] together in [your] mother's womb" (Psalm 139:13). Tell your mom that I don't want no smoke with her before she comes at me saying, "I spent twenty-five hours in labor for that child." No, I want to give her honor where honor is due. Yes, it is true that she and your father conceived you. Yes, she carried you for many months in her womb. Yes, she spent x number of hours in labor. Yes, her body was altered and possibly irreversibly damaged in the process of your birth.

But, with all due respect (anytime someone says that--watch out!), all she did (and I say that very loosely) was deliver you. She was a trusted vessel of developing and delivering, but God designed you! The entire birth process from conception through development and delivery was orchestrated by God. My point in saying these things is not for you to attack or belittle your parents, but to free you from any shame concerning how you may have come into this world.

This book is titled, *Out of the Ashes: Finding the Purpose in Your Pain,* however, before we can truly delve into your purpose, the pain that many may have buried for years must be unpacked and addressed. You cannot build anything on a faulty foundation and expect it to stand the test of time. This reminds me of a story in the Bible.

> 24 "Therefore everyone who hears these words of mine and puts them into practice is like a wise man who built his house on the rock. 25 The rain came down, the streams rose, and the winds blew and beat against that house; yet it did not fall, because it had its foundation on the rock. 26 But everyone who hears these words of mine and does not put them into practice is like a foolish man who built his house on sand. 27 The rain came down, the streams rose, and the winds blew and beat against that house, and it fell with a great crash." **Matthew 7:24-27 (NLT)**

As an educator, I have had the privilege of working with some of the best teachers in the world; but Jesus is still the very best in my opinion. What made him so great is that He always taught in parables so anyone, from a young child to a seasoned adult, could understand. In this parable, His analogy speaks to the fallacy of building one's life on anything but God's Word and how detrimental it can be if someone makes that choice. He is using a physical house to personify our lives and the rains, streams, and wind to symbolize the calamity and adversity in life. Only a solid foundation can withstand those forces physically, and the same holds true spiritually.

In the same way, how we perceive the genesis of our existence is the foundation of our lives. When we have doubts about our worth or even question whether or not we should be alive, it's like the person who built their life on sand, and when the storms of life come—not *if*, but *when* — there is little chance that their foundation will remain secure. My personal foundation is my belief in Christ, and I strive to build my life upon His Word. I know some people view the Bible as some old, dusty, irrelevant (and possibly not true) book, but I believe it IS true and has wisdom for every situation we encounter. (And for those of you who like reality shows, binge watching TV series on streaming platforms, or like dramatic films, the Bible is chock full of some of the most entertaining true stories to say the least.) Hebrews 4:12 says, "For the word of God is alive and active..." Basically, this means that even though the biblical text was written centuries ago, it still applies to us and is relevant for us today.

Still don't think so?

Imagine having the opportunity to live in a beautiful glass condo in the San Francisco Bay Area overlooking the city with panoramic views. Well, for residents of the Millennium Tower, this was not merely a dream, it was their daily reality. Constructed in 2008, the building had amenities including a movie theater, fitness center, wine cellar and tasting room, pool, and concierge service. One of the more notable residents was Joe Montana, a four-time Super Bowl champion who was a quarterback for the San Francisco 49ers and Kansas City Chiefs. This tower appeared to be the next great wonder of the world and a lucrative real estate asset. Until it wasn't.

In 2010, just two years after construction was completed, it was discovered that the building was sinking. All structures settle; that is normal. What alarmed consultants was the rate at which the Millennium Tower was sinking—four inches more than what was anticipated. There are theories floating around about the cause of this abnormal rate of sinking, with the most common cause consisting of two components: 1) the depth, and 2) the foundation material. The building's foundation was only eighty feet down, and it was built on packed sand.

Truly wise people prefer to learn from the mistakes of others rather than their own. Millennium Partners, the developers of the Millennium Tower, are facing countless lawsuits from hundreds of people in the millions of dollars because of a lack of intentionality when choosing the foundation on which to construct their building. A massive 645-foot-tall, 400-unit, $350 million edifice is all but useless now for two simple reasons: a lack of depth, and a lack of substance. The Millennium Tower is a beautiful and expensive building, but it cannot compare to the value and beauty that God sees in you, His creation.

I have two questions for you:

1. What is the foundation of your identity and of your life composed of?

2. How deep does your foundation go?

The last thing you want is to build a wonderful life on a faulty foundation. Imagine going to college, starting your career or trade, meeting the love of your life, starting a family only to have it all fall apart because you never dealt with the pain of your past. That would be much more tragic than the story of the Millennium Tower.

One principle that is woven throughout the Bible is that it is never too late for God to turn your situation around. It is never too late to be used by Him. As humans, we are bound and restricted by time, but God can move through time at will. Whether or not you have come to grips with how you entered the world, or have never even thought about it, if you are reading this it is not too late!

"This song is dedicated to people like me. Those who struggle with insecurities, acceptance, and even low self-esteem. You never felt good enough. You never felt pretty enough. But imagine God whispering in your ear and letting you know everything that happened is all gone."
-"Imagine Me" by Kirk Franklin

I dedicate this book to people like me. I have struggled with all of the things above and more myself.

Depression. Check.

Self-esteem. Check.

Identity issues. Check.

Anxiety. Check.

As a well-known saying goes, the journey of a thousand miles begins with one step, and the first step is usually the hardest one.

I am excited for you as you embark on this journey of self-discovery and healing. As you read through this book, I will share personal stories from my life, wisdom I have gathered along the way, and equip you with tools to propel you into your purpose. In order to build a life that can withstand the rain, streams, winds and storms of life, you must have a proper view of ourself: that is your solid foundation. This starts with believing one truth:

You are **not** an accident!

I dare you to find a mirror or pull out your phone, look into the camera and tell yourself, "(Say your name), you are **not** an accident!!!"

Chapter 2

EMBRACE YOUR ORIGINS

"Never forget where you came from, but always remember where you're going"

"God, what were you thinking?! I mean were You thinking at all?!!"

God can handle your anger, trust me. And it does not matter whether we have given ourselves permission to voice our disdain towards God for the way our life has unfolded, we have all been at this place before. It is perfectly fine to question things that have happened to you and even tell God you're upset with him. I mean He is God. He already knows anyway, right?

I want you to understand one thing about me as a person and even the manner in which I have approached writing this book:

> I acknowledge the harsh realities of life while still hoping for improbable possibilities.

If I am being completely honest, I aspire to be a glass half-full type of person, but most of the time I am warring against my natural tendency to see it half empty. The one thing that helps me come to grips with many things is holding onto the truth that I shared with you earlier:

Two things can be true at the same time.

Life becomes much more peaceful when we allow ourselves to accept the dualities of life instead of fighting against them. Our desire to make sense of things and gain understanding of the world around us causes us to take a brush and paint the world black and white. The elephant in the room is this: life is full of "gray" areas (and so is the elephant for that matter). Take your life as an example.

Maybe Chapter 1 was not for you. You may never have struggled with believing you were not an accident. Maybe you have struggled in the past, but after reading the first chapter, you have fully embraced the intentionality with which God created you. It is one thing to accept how you came into the world, it is another thing entirely to face the world into which you came.

"If God loves me so much, and I'm chosen by Him, why would he allow me to be born into poverty?"

"Why would God allow me to be born into a household of abuse?"

"Why did I have to witness drug addiction growing up?"

These and other questions about home environments and upbringing trouble the minds of people all over the world.

How can I be chosen by God, but also have no choice in how I was conceived, who my parents are, or where and when I was born? If God really loved me, surely He never would have allowed me to have to deal with some of these problems.

Part of the healing process is realizing that you are not alone in your struggle. I, too, have wondered the same things.

Before I delve into more of my background, I want to preface what I am about to share with this statement:

I love my family.

I know they raised me the best way they could.

I do not blame them for everything that is wrong with me.

It is not my intent to harm anyone I know by sharing about my personal life.

With all of that being said and with all due respect (uh-oh), this is my story to tell and my truth to share. The Bible says, "Then you will know the truth, and the truth will set you free" John 8:32 (NIV). Many of us live our lives based on lies because sometimes the truth hurts. If you ask the residents of the Millennium Tower, it would have been much more bearable to discover the truth about their building sooner rather than later. If telling the truth makes you question your loyalty to others, I have some exciting news for you:

Loyalty is overrated.

I discovered this while hearing a sermon one Sunday morning by Pastor Eric D. Lacy. Pastor E, went on to say that

being loyal is problematic because it will cause you to ignore character flaws in the one who is the object of your loyalty, for the sake of not "betraying" them.

You don't have to throw the ones you love under the bus in order to share your perspective about what growing up was like for you. In addition to this, you do not need to pretend that everything was okay while hiding the damage that was done.

Things are not always mutually exclusive. I can appreciate my parents for not aborting me when they could have, while also hating the struggles we faced financially as a result of their young parenthood. I am not here to paint myself as a martyr and make my situation appear to be worse than what it was for the sake of receiving pity. My parents were young, but they had support from both sides of their families with raising me and my siblings. For the most part, I had what I needed growing up, but that doesn't mean there were times when I did not. I received new clothes and shoes, but I also wore hand-me-downs. I was never malnourished or starved, but there were times when money was tight, my lunch account at school was negative, and I was hungry.

Acknowledging that the good in your life outweighs the bad, does not take away the bad things that really did happen. Addressing the bad does not cancel the good things either. They can both exist simultaneously.

Can we really apply this truth to every situation? Yes!

One of the things that is true of the family that I was born into is that there is a history of mental illness.

September 3, 2004 is the worst day of my life! No other day is even close!

Why?

It was on that day that I awoke to an eerie sound echoing through the hallway between my parents' room and mine. I heard screaming and yelling, but that was not unusual because my parents would argue like any other couple would--but this was different.

As I approached the threshold of their bedroom, my 11-year-old eyes widened to the size of the sun and fear consumed my body: my father was assaulting my mother!

With the weight of his body balanced between both knees, straddling her back, he held both of her arms as if they were the handles of a wheelbarrow and repeatedly drove her face into the carpet. He only paused long enough for her to catch her breath as she pleaded for him to stop:

"What about your son?!"

"Let me say bye to my son!"

"Aaaaah!"

"Daddy stop! Please stop!" I begged him.

He told me to go to my room.

I ran to my bed and curled myself into the fetal position, filled with terror. I don't recall the exact words, but I began to pray.

"Grab the phone and call for help," I thought.

I darted out of my room and grabbed our black wireless house phone only to realize the battery was missing. It must have been lost in whatever scuffle preceded what was now happening. I laid there a few moments more, curled into a ball, teary-eyed, and feeling utterly and completely helpless as I listened to more pleas and shrieks from my mother as her life hung in the balance.

I realized I was at a fork in the road: I could lie there and just accept this as my fate or I could take action to affect the situation.

Although I was scared out of my mind, I mustered up the courage to run out of our front door and bolt down the street to my grandparents' home. When I arrived at their front door, my heart was beating out of my chest. My grandmother walked with me as I headed back to our home.

Embrace Your Origins

When we arrived, a neighbor and my grandfather were already there and had helped to de-escalate the situation. The cops arrived, arrested my father, and escorted him out in handcuffs. The images of that night left a mark on me forever.

... I think the city that we're from just kinda ruined things. It's such a small place, not much to do but talk and listen.

-Drake

What made matters worse was growing up in a small town. This was all printed in various newspapers. Not that it really mattered because in places like my hometown "it's not much to do but talk and listen." Word travels fast! There are many benefits to this: it kept many kids out of trouble, it provided safety, it helped to build a sense of community, and it kept people connected.

There were also a ton of drawbacks: it encouraged gossip, people felt like they knew you based on what they heard about you, and when ANYTHING happened, good or bad, everyone knew in a matter of hours. This was even before the rise of social media.

The greatest pains of my life were harvested from the seeds of this horrific night.

My father received treatment and eventually returned home. He was never a violent person, and that was not the norm in our household. Sure there were arguments, and elevated voices, but never to this degree. I believe that is what made it so traumatic for me.

> Fear began to be the lens that filtered everything I saw in my life.

I always admired my mother's courage, forgiveness, resiliency, and determination to keep our family together. Personally, I'm not so sure I would have returned, and even if I were to return, it would not be as soon as she did. I was not ready, and I believe that got lost in translation. I do not blame her because there was so much going on during that time, but it weighed on me heavily.

What is sleep?

This was the beginning of nearly a decade of insufferable insomnia for me.

The first few years after the attack, the entire event replayed in my dreams in vivid high-definition - that is, when I did sleep.

The fear of it repeating itself consumed me.

I could not allow myself to get caught off guard again - my very life could depend on it.

I would literally stay awake until my body betrayed me with fatigue. It was somewhat intentional and also out of my control at the same time. The irony was that while I was asleep, it was the only time I experienced peace; but the terror that plagued me would not allow me to rest for long.

At the root of it all was a desire to be in control at all times.

My fear drove me to never "get caught off guard" again. I believed I suffered from PTSD as a result of witnessing this horrific incident. The trauma caused me to be on high alert as a form of self-preservation. I always wanted to be in a position to protect myself - AT ALL TIMES!!! Home is supposed to be your safe haven. If you do not feel peace at home with the ones that you love, where can you possibly hope to find it elsewhere?

I am not looking for your pity. I appreciate any sympathy I may receive as a result of sharing my life with you, but that was not the point of me opening up about this painful part of my past. I am a huge fan of Michael Todd, pastor of Transformation Church in Tulsa, Oklahoma. One of his

Embrace Your Origins

catch phrases is, "We are a 'H.O.T.' church: Humble, Open and Transparent." Rather than having you **sympathize** with me; **I want to empathize with you.**

"You don't know my story,

All the things that I've been through;

You can't feel my pain,

What I had to go through to get here

-"My Worship is For Real"

by Bishop Larry Trotter & Sweet Holy Spirit

I do not pretend to understand what you have been through. No matter how similar our lives may be, there is no one exactly like you in this entire world: you are one of a kind. One thing I do know is that you have been through something.

Every human on this planet is a flawed individual. Ever since Adam & Eve disobeyed God, sin has been in our DNA and has continued to be passed down for generations. How do I know this? You do not have to teach a child to behave badly. You do not have to teach a baby to be selfish. It cries and cries until its needs are met regardless of how it interferes with the needs of those around it. This means that our families, friends, colleagues, communities, cities and this world are full of people with character flaws and negative traits. Do we all have good and redeeming qualities too? Yes! But the existence of the good does not negate the presence of the bad.

Why is all of this relevant?

I am glad you asked!

The world into which you were born is full of sin and evil. This means that no matter how much your family loves you, they are bound to hurt you from time to time. Just because you don't mean to hurt someone that doesn't take away from their pain.

I want to make it clear that I love my father. I have for-given my father. I would not be the man I am today without his presence in my life. As a child, he would pray with me every night and his example instilled a desire and passion for Christ. However, his battle with mental illness left me with some scars.

Up until that night, I would say that my dad was a model citizen of what a man should be. He provided, protected, and set the spiritual climate of our home. I learned so much by just being in his presence and observing how he carried himself and treated others. He was the type of person to give you the shirt off of his back. Prior to this time period, my dad coached me in basketball, attended anything I was involved in after school, and was always there. I hesitated using the word was, but the reality is, that some days I felt like a fatherless child.

[Fred Hammond:]

There's a hole in my soul

That won't heal

And there's a rage and a pain

Even now I still feel

And even though I'm a man

Still I don't understand

But that's what happens

When you don't have a father

That's what happens

When you don't have a father

"Interlude #1" Kirk Franklin feat. Fred Hammond

A father or mother can be physically present and yet still be absent from a child's life. We always equate absentee parenthood with people who are not there in a physical sense. But actually "being there" for your son or daughter in an emotional sense is an entirely different matter. I want everyone reading this to understand that my father has a real mental illness that he continues to battle, so it was not his intention to not be there in the way I needed him. Yet, the fact still remains that I felt abandoned at the beginning of one of the most critical parts of my development in life— adolescence.

Gradually, his presence began to fade from my life. When I would look into the stands at my football and basketball games, my track meets and academic competitions, and Youth & Government conferences, he wouldn't be there. I began to develop what could be called a "thick skin."

"The opposite of love is not hate; it's indifference."

I did in fact experience a period of time in which I felt like I hated my father.

> My hate was really my love for him coated in painful disappointment.

Eventually, it was too draining to feel hatred towards him because hate is still an emotion and it took too much out of me to carry that on a daily basis. Eventually I settled in on indifference. *He can't hurt me if I don't care*, I would think to myself.

My indifference was just a callous that was beginning to form around my heart. The dictionary says a callous is "a thickened and hardened part of the skin in an area that has been subject to friction." The body forms this new tissue to protect itself in an area that has been wounded previously. I didn't want to feel the pain of his absence, so I just completely shielded myself from it by pretending not to care. Eventually, for a period of time, I really believe I didn't care anymore.

As painful as September 3rd was for me, the years to follow were probably much worse. As I progressed through my life, I grew accustomed to my father not being there for me or my siblings either physically or emotionally. As much as I had hardened myself in an effort to ignore my suffering, it was affecting me more than I realized at the time. Looking back, I did not realize the magnitude of the toll it was starting to take on me.

Anytime I hit a major milestone, it was always bittersweet because a war raged within me between my indifference and my love for my father. It was kind of like the scenes in those movies where a person has an angel on one shoulder and a devil on the other. The two of them are giving opposing forms of counsel to advise you on a dilemma you're facing. On the one hand, I didn't want him to show up to these events because of all of the built-up resentment hidden under the façade of indifference I maintained. Secondly, I could never be sure how he would conduct himself in that moment, and I didn't want what I was doing to be tainted by something he did. On the other hand,

> the little boy in me yearned for the presence, adoration and affirmation that only a father could bring.

The last major milestone that my dad witnessed was my high school graduation. However, since then there have been several critical moments in my life that he missed. Teaching me to drive. Learning how to tie a tie. My first sermon—or any sermon in person. My college graduation. And even my wedding.

When a father is not present physically, emotionally, or fails to provide, it leaves a void in that child. Fortunately for me, I had other men in my life who have stepped up and stood in the gap for me as father figures, but they were only substitutes at best. The illustration I use to paint this picture

Embrace Your Origins

is the difference between a dollar bill and the many ways it can be converted to change. A father is to a dollar bill as an uncle, or grandfather, or other relatives is to a quarter, dime, nickel or penny. Yes, it is true that four quarters are the same as one dollar. One hundred pennies have the same value as a dollar. Ten dimes will buy just as much as a dollar bill will, but there are also differences. A dollar bill is more portable, more potent and more efficient. It's also so much lighter than the coins of the same value. Yes, the coins may have the same worth, but someone has to carry the extra weight. That someone was me.

What I'm really saying is that no one else in your life can ever truly replace the void left by an absent parent or fill the space a child holds for a parent in their heart, no matter who that parent is. My uncles and grandfather and other men in my life did an excellent job of making me feel like I was their son. Honestly, there were moments when I truly felt that way—but then reality would smack me right in the face. Whenever I would see them interact with their actual sons or fathers, resentment, jealousy, and envy would sometimes begin to manifest itself in my spirit. Many times this would challenge my faith and trust in God.

"God, why do I have to suffer like this?!"

But God promises that He is "A father to the fatherless..."
-Psalm 68:5

By God's grace, my father's struggle, and his resulting absence, pushed me into a deeper relationship with Him (Jesus). I had no alternative but to rely on my Heavenly Father to fulfill the needs left unfulfilled by my earthly one. Remember when I said I felt hatred towards my dad at one point? That period of time was the summer before my tenth-grade year. I didn't realize it at the time, but that year would be a pivotal one in my life spiritually.

School was always my escape and safe haven, so having to stay home during the summer was always agonizing to me. I always utilized sports, after school activities, and just the day-to-day grind of school to take my mind off of my new life of insomnia, fear and anxiety. Going from being away eight hours or more each day to now being home 24/7 was almost insufferable. The time and space school provided was a buffer for my burdens. I would normally only have to manage a few hours of dealing with my home life, but now I had to find a way to make it through an entire day for nearly three months.

It couldn't get any worse than this right?!

Except it did!

I don't know exactly when it started, but it got to a point that I felt like my father was intentionally trying to antagonize me. It would always be something trivial that seemed to be just a ploy to try to get a reaction from me. Before we left for summer break, my ninth-grade math teacher gave me a stack of magazines that featured prominent professional Christian athletes. They always had at least one poster you could tear out and hang up in your room. I drew a lot of inspiration from these magazines, and they were a source of hope and peace for me.

I began to hang the posters all over the walls of my room not knowing it would become a source of contention between me and my father. My first attempt at putting them up was to use tape, but my father disapproved because he said it could rip the paint off of the wall. *No biggie*, I thought to myself. I would just find some tacks and use those instead of the tape. Then, upon discovering my new method, he told me to take them down because the tacks would put holes in the walls. I wish this were the only example of this type of behavior—but there are more examples.

My dad was always getting on me about my grades because he demanded academic excellence. I did not always approve of his methods (In ninth grade, I was once grounded for making an 89.4), but overall, I respect what he was doing. And now as an adult, even if I still don't always agree with how he went about it, I know it came from a place of love and always wanting me to do my absolute best so I could have great opportunities in my future. When I finally brought up my grades to all A's, he got me a cell phone. Unfortunately, hard times arose, and I assume the bill became too high, so my cell phone was cut off towards the end of my ninth-grade school year.

Even though I couldn't text or call anyone, I would still use the phone in the summer as a way of getting me through those difficult and lonely days. The phone had a feature on it that allowed it to pick up radio stations using the headphones as an antenna. From my room, I couldn't pick up my normal go-to favorite stations, but I discovered a few that I did enjoy and being able to have that provide some sort of enjoyment was better than nothing. Unfortunately, this did not last long.

Without any warning or explanation, my dad came into my room one day and asked me to give him the phone. This was absolutely my breaking point. I was used to his academic expectations and knew that it always came from a good place, but the posters and cell phone situation was something different. I took those situations as personal attacks on my joy. I didn't have much of a social life at the time and didn't have too many things that truly made me happy, so to take away the few things that did bring me any sort of positive emotion was deadening. A switch flipped in my spirit and I entered into a dark headspace.

From that day onward, my father became my enemy. I took the passion of my love for him and inverted it, added a little anger, resentment, bitterness, sprinkled a dash of indifference, and created a recipe for disaster pertaining to my relationship with him. What ensued over the next few weeks of that summer was utter spiritual darkness in our home.

The saying goes, "Keep your friends close and your enemies closer," but I chose to keep this enemy—my dad—distant. I developed a strategy to completely withdraw all expressions of love or adoration towards him. I deliberately decided to speak to him only when absolutely necessary. Our house was not very large by any standard, but when we would pass each other, I would not speak. We would make brief eye contact and go our separate ways. If he asked me a question, I would answer. If he asked me to do something, I would do it. He just lost any and all small talk or conversation just for the sake of conversing. It was not necessarily my goal to anger him, but it began to weigh on him and eventually it came to a head one day.

I was playing football at the time and wanted to work out to earn a starting spot on the junior varsity team. My father's truck was out of commission, and during this time period he wasn't normally doing these types of things anyway, so I waited until my mother got home to ask her about taking me to the fieldhouse and track to start working out. This infuriated him, but not just for the obvious reasons.

Looking forward to my mother coming home from work was how I got through many days during this time. She'd come back with snacks from the commissary (she works at a prison), groceries, or maybe a bucket of fried chicken from time to time. On a side note, I was already using food to cope during this time and would eat up all the snacks she would buy for us way too fast—sorry Momma. But, most importantly, her presence alone was enough to just bring another wave of energy to the house. We didn't even have to speak, but just knowing she was there and not having to bear the weight of this dark cloud of negativity alone was everything to me. I would talk to her as soon as she walked in and my demeanor was different towards her. This is what

Embrace Your Origins

I truly believe caused my father to grow more and more angry over time.

Back to the day of the workout incident: I remember him coming into the living room and saying to me, "If you ever sit up here all day and ask your mother something you could've asked me, you're..." I honestly don't remember verbatim what he said after that, but it basically alluded to me receiving some sort of punishment. Even as a teen, I had enough awareness to know this had absolutely nothing to do with the situation that was being addressed. My request to my mother about working out was just a cover for the real issue—it bothered him to see me show so much enthusiasm in seeing my mom come home when I hadn't shown him any all day. At that moment, the proverbial final nail was placed in the coffin. He may have been living, but he was dead to me.

You cannot make someone love you. You cannot coerce, punish or use fear to influence that choice. Their love for you or lack thereof is a decision they make independent of you. The Bible directly addresses this also. John 4:18 says:

"There is no fear in love. But perfect love drives out fear because fear has to do with punishment. The one who fears is not made perfect in love."

The most a person can hope to do with fear is to make someone say they love them. They may even force them to behave as if they appear to love them, but true love is a conscious choice that an individual must make on their own.

Several times in my adolescence, I contemplated running away—this was one of those times. I have since told my family, but I don't know if they ever realized the magnitude of that statement or the depth to which I had thought this out. I had family in a small town about 20 minutes away. *I could reach out to them and let them help me*, I would think to myself. *But surely the police would come and look for you there, then what? Are you gonna make them lie to the police and risk jail time for you? What about your education? What about college?* This little speck of hope in the distant future and the legal implications of running away are literally what kept me from acting on it. But I was running out of hope. I was reaching my breaking point. Thank God for my extended family.

At one point, much of my family all lived in Palestine, Texas together. There was a time when my family, my aunt and her family, my uncle and his family and my grandparents all lived on the same street. At this point everyone had moved to the Houston area except for us. They would visit throughout the year as my uncle and grandfather still owned property, but it wasn't quite the same as all of us growing up living on the same street. Even from a distance, I knew we still had their support.

I thank God for my extended family because their attentiveness toward me saved my life. Many times during the summer, they would come and take me with them back to Houston just so I could get out of the house. My aunt would sometimes take me to see semi-professional football games. My uncle would let me come to his house and hang out with my other cousins, and sometimes we would go help him pass out flyers for his real estate business. My grandfather would have me organize things on his computer, add programs or even do yard work. His house was in the country and his yard was huge. The front and back together was like a football field at least—maybe a little smaller than that. Quite frankly, I really didn't care if they had me work every day all summer; that would have been a small price to pay for peace. Peace is priceless.

I didn't realize it, but they had noticed there was something going on with me long before I did. Outwardly, I had obvious red flags: I walked with my head down, I was timid, I clearly lacked confidence. That wasn't necessarily out of the ordinary for the average teenager though. My uncle also told me he would wake up in the middle of the night having dreams about me and worrying if I was okay. My aunt was formerly a teacher at the school district where I was attending school before she moved, so she was still in touch with people there. Several students would tell her that they worried about me from what they had observed me do. But one post I made on social media completely changed my life.

Before we had the popular apps of today, there was this thing called Myspace. I made a post on there once that said, "Surrounded by people but feel alone." I don't remember the exact date when I made the post, but I do remember the moment when I did it very clearly. I honestly wasn't seeking attention or anything, I just used my page to express myself and that is how I felt. Just like they always say, "Be careful what you post on the Internet because you never know who might see it." Thank God much of my family were friends on that account and saw it and discussions began concerning how they could help me.

In the middle of the summer, I spent some extended time with my uncle and his family. When I say extended, I mean that what was supposed to be a week turned into several because every time he asked me if I wanted to go home, I would say, "Not yet." Eventually, school and two-a-days for football were approaching and it was out of my hands, but he had called back home to some family friends and made arrangements for me to get a ride to and from practice because he knew how much of an outlet football was for me. He even spoke to my father on my behalf about making sure I got to practice because it meant a lot to me. This gave me hope that things were starting to change.

A major change was on the horizon, but it didn't come in the way that I thought. The first day I was supposed to join the carpool was going great. My dad woke up early with me and even made sure I had breakfast. Everything was going according to plan, until I heard someone blow their car horn. *It's my ride!* I thought, but not showing any signs of my excitement outwardly. My dad went out and told them to leave. He told them that he would take me. Internally I questioned the validity of this because I knew his truck was not running at the time. It doesn't take a rocket scientist to figure out that I didn't end up going to practice that day. This process repeated itself a few times until eventually my ride just stopped coming to get me.

"You intended to harm me, but God intended it for good to accomplish what is now being done, the saving of many lives."
Genesis 50:20 NIV

What seemed like a burden at the time was about to turn into a blessing. Remember those posters that I couldn't tape or tack on the wall? Instead of worrying about the posters, I just started reading the magazines. The magazines were filled with inspirational stories of Christian athletes, devotionals and scriptures. The more I read them and began to fill my mind with something positive, I began to notice a change within myself. In a moment I had with God, I prayed,

"God if you're not going to take me out of this situation, then give me the strength to deal with it."

I softened my heart towards my father and began to pray for him. In no way were we best friends at this point, but I did let go of the bitterness and just gave it to God. He still was hurting me and disappointing me, but I didn't try to take it upon myself to punish him, judge him or seek revenge. I kid you not, not long after I prayed this prayer, something surreal happened next.

I would say that no longer than two weeks after praying that prayer, my uncle and his wife came to visit. After coming inside and speaking to everyone, my dad and mom left

Embrace Your Origins

with the both of them and were gone for about an hour or so. This was strange because they didn't normally do this, but I didn't think much of it at the time. I remember lying on my bed when I heard a knock at the door. It was my mom and she told me to pack my things because I was going with my uncle. That's literally all she said, but my gut told me this meant something different. I packed all of the clothes I had and got into the car with them and left.

We stopped in town at a burger place with golden arches. As we sat at the table, they informed me of what was going on and asked me if I was okay with going with them. I told them that I was okay with it. Then they asked me again, explaining that this wouldn't be a visit, but that I would be moving in with them, and again I said, "Yes."

It was almost like God was waiting on me to embrace where I was before he could change what was going on in my environment. All of that time before I was contemplating how to run away, praying to be taken away, and even just wishing not to have to wake up some mornings. The moment I began to trust God and just give this situation over to him was the moment He began to work things out in my favor.

What has happened to you in your life that you have yet to embrace?

Is it the family into which you were born?

The neighborhood in which you grew up.

The horrible things you witnessed as a child.

Embracing your origins is not about learning to like the negative situations you've endured; it's about accepting them as part of your story. You are the sum total of everything you've been through—good and bad. We have this fantasy in our minds about wanting to erase some of the bad things that have happened to us because we think we would have turned out better, but what would have changed in the process?

If you've seen any movie about time travel, they all have one thing in common: if you change one small, seemingly insignificant thing, the entire story changes. In some films it has been said that even leaving a piece of trash behind could alter the universe. When a character changes one interaction in an effort to make the future better, it could even cause someone not to exist later on. Have you ever thought about that?

What if you had your way and could go back and change something about your past?

Sounds exciting, right?

Before you start romanticizing the idea of that—that's easy—I want you to think about the alternative. What would change about you if you did that? Would you still have the same strength? Would you still have the same wisdom? Would you like or even recognize this new version of yourself?

Unfortunately for us, just like being born, we had no choice concerning the families we were born into. We had no say in the city or cities we grew up in. Many terrible things have happened to us that were out of our control, but we aren't helpless victims without any hope. We all have a choice!

> God, grant me the serenity to accept the things I cannot change, courage to change the things I can, and wisdom to know the difference.
> -Reinhold Niebuhr

There is another version of this prayer that asks for courage first, and I started to add that one, but then it dawned on me that there is a necessary sequence that must take place. None of us can skip to courage without acceptance first. Many of us want the courage to change our future without embracing the past. Once again, it's not about looking at the past with rose-colored glasses, but it is about acknowledging what happened and coming to grips with it.

What about your past do you need to embrace in order to move forward?

What is something that you have the ability to change in your present circumstance?

Say this, "My worst days are behind me, and my best days are ahead of me!"

Chapter 3

REMOVE THE LABELS

"You live for their acceptance you die from their rejection-
"Free From It All" by Lecrae

Who are you?

I am willing to bet, the first thing that comes to your mind when you introduce yourself is your name. Your name is very significant. It is a major part of who you are—key word **part**—but it's simply an identifier.

So again, I ask, "Who are you?"

If I was initially wrong about how you responded to this question the first time, you may have stated your occupation.

"I am a teacher at such and such school."

"I am a freelance photographer."

"I am an auto mechanic."

Whatever industry you work in, whether you view your occupation as just a job to pay the bills, a career, or even if it is your passion—it is still something that you do. Your job does not and should not define who you are.

So, the question remains:

Who are you?

Out of desperation, you find the closest mirror, gaze at the person staring back at you and you have an epiphany. You notice the hue of your skin and conclude that you are your race or ethnicity.

"I am black"

"I am Asian"

"I am Puerto Rican."

"I'm Irish."

Race is an enigma. My junior year of high school, I had a phenomenal AP US History teacher, and he taught me a life-altering concept that I will never forget:

Race is a social construct!

In my opinion, there is only one race—the human race. This is backed by science as there is not enough genetic variation to truly support the practice of separating people according to the way the world views race. Essentially, race is a man-made system in order to classify people. Another reason why this is confusing is because people often use the words *race* and *ethnicity* interchangeably.

Race and ethnicity are not the same. Race is focused on biology and physical characteristics such as skin, eye, and hair color. Ethnicity is based upon cultural expression and identification. A person could physically appear to be of one race yet be a part of an entirely different culture. This is just one example that shows the fallacy of this system in which we live.

Now, back to reality.

Unfortunately, race as a socially constructed notion does not refute the reality in which we live. Although science and common-sense thinking can prove that this is true, it does not change the fact that a majority of the world sees me as a black man. The way I am perceived by the world comes with a different set of expectations depending on the environment in which I find myself in a given moment. This causes some to fear me, others to hate me, and many to love me all the more, but it still isn't entirely who I am.

Names. Occupations. Race. Ethnicity. What do they all have in common? They are all labels given to us in an effort to define or classify us. These classifications are society's way of trying to make sense of the differences between us all. When someone cannot come to grips with the differences, fear and rejection are soon to follow.

"What's understood ain't gotta be explained/But you don't understand me so let me explain."
- "Misunderstood" by Lil Wayne

I don't know about you, but much of my life I have felt misunderstood. Growing up, I never truly found a place or group that I felt fully embraced ALL of me for who I was. This reminds me of an interview I listened to by Andy Mineo from his album, *Work in Progress*.

"I think as humans, we like boxes. It helps us understand the world quicker. If I can just put you in this box, I can understand things. And uh—you know that's been something we've always fought against: to break out of boxes. Cause people are not homogenous, they don't all think the same, they don't all have the exact same workings as people—someone—who may look like them.

And so to unbox the world is to make it a lot less controlled.

Remove the Labels

And I think we love control. We love to think we're in control or at least think, 'I understand these people, I can see through this.'

> However, you don't leave room for people to be complex or to be unique.

And if you're willing to box other people in like that quickly, you're probably not doing the work on yourself to understand who you are."

There is so much to unpack in this quote! (No pun intended). We all have been on both sides of this: putting others in boxes and being put in a box by other people. I remember hearing that quote for the first time and instantly connecting to what he was saying and seeing myself in what he was articulating.

As I stated earlier, I have often felt misunderstood, and due to an unwillingness by some not to make the effort to get to know me as an individual, people would take the lazy route and just stick a label on me and put me into one of their boxes.

Has this ever happened to you?

Growing up there were so many labels put on me and boxes I was placed in. Due to my height and hue, there was always this expectation placed upon my shoulders to be super athletic—but I never was. Due to my intelligence, I was placed in classes with people who could match me on an academic level, but rarely reflected people who could relate to my cultural experience. I've been called a nerd for the way I crave knowledge— and I can't really refute that one. It was and still is pretty applicable to me if I'm being honest. Kobe even said he was a nerd for basketball, it's just that basketball is something that is more socially acceptable to be a nerd about. I have been one of few blacks in advanced placement classes to whom everyone who wasn't black turned for knowledge of all things black. Even my "blackness" was questioned countless times because of my unathletic nerdiness. If that's all it took to not be black, then we wouldn't have so many hashtags in honor of so many people of color who have fallen unjustly. I was even labeled as an overall lame person, but that one I actually agree with.

I **was** so lame!

Yes, I **was** lame! I'm really emphasizing **was**, but I wanna be humble, open and transparent as Michael Todd says, so I gotta keep it a hunnit! (100% authentic) But what was it about me that would cause me to agree with this statement?

Was it my clothes?

No. But, I used to wear some awful ensembles. The glow up is real!

Was it the fact that I wasn't that great of an athlete?

Nah, but I had room for improvement. A lot of room!

Maybe it was because I wasn't "black enough"?

My being black is not even a choice, so why would I let someone else define it for me?

Then what was it that made me feel like they were right about me being lame?

All of those aforementioned things about me are all true, but none of those are why I believe I was lame. I wasn't lame for any of the reasons people may have thought. Most of those things were out of my control anyway. This is why I believe:

I was lame for allowing how I thought others perceived me to occupy any amount of space in my mind.

I was even more lame for allowing their perceptions of me to affect my decision-making. This was a very harmful habit. This mindset would later come back to haunt me.

All of those labels were relatively mild in nature. I'm not gonna sit here and lie by saying they didn't bother me, but there was one label that bothered me the most. Those were annoying and a little irritating, but this one wounded me on a deeper level.

Growing up, it was my goal to save myself for marriage and remain abstinent until then. I wasn't shy about telling someone when the topic of sex came up, and I was very vocal about why I believed this was what was best for me. Looking back, I would keep the same fire, zeal and conviction, but I would have chosen my declarations much more carefully when it came to when I was speaking about it. In many ways, I made it much harder on myself by placing a huge target on my back, but regardless of how I handled it, kids were going to be kids. The way I looked at it was, I might as well own it because they're gonna talk about me regardless. I just think I was a tad bit overzealous.

The teasing about not having sex didn't bother me too much because I was really convicted about it, and I knew my reasons. I wanted to be wealthy one day and knew having children prematurely would make that aspiration much harder. I knew what it was like growing up with money being tight and not getting to do everything I wanted to because of that. My most impassioned reason was wanting to have all of my children live with me in the same house and have them all share the same mother. Growing up, I dealt with having a sister who had a different father, and a sister who had a different mother, and it was tough. One I grew up with until I was about eight, and then we never lived in the same house again after that. The other sister never lived with us and was only allowed to visit sporadically. This was something I thought about on an almost daily basis and that kept me focused on my goal.

> But anything worth doing is going to be hard because if it were easy, everyone would do it.

"See where I'm from they call you gay

Say you ain't a man, show them you ain't no punk

Get all the girls you can, a simple plan that still haunts me even now today..."

"Let It Go" -Kirk Franklin

In case you haven't guessed it by now, the label that people put on me that cut the deepest was accusing me of being gay. As the song says, where I'm from that is one of the worst things you could be called. Before someone gets online and calls for me to be cancelled, at least hear me out. (My intention in bringing this up isn't to offend anyone, but to explain what I was going through at the time. I have certain convictions about this based on biblical principles, but this book isn't about getting into this issue.)

Somehow, by the grace of God, I left high school never having had sex. However, my resolve was beginning to dull on the issue. Although I grew up in church, and the people around me said they supported what I was trying to do, I didn't personally know anyone else—especially males— who were consciously trying to do what I was doing. Let me add this too:

Remaining celibate was a choice.

As broken as I was, as insecure as I was at the time, the enemy still presented me with opportunities to fail. But once again, many people wouldn't expect that because I had already been labeled.

Ahh, college!

Remove the Labels

This was my chance to start over, or so I thought.

I was much more confident than I was when I first moved to Houston. Although I never went to professional therapy, the move proved to be therapeutic. Between hanging around cousins in my age group, being closer to more of my extended family, and being mentored by my grandfather and uncle, I had healed and grown a lot—just not as much as I thought.

My first semester of college, I had one major goal: **don't go home!** I had heard and personally witnessed countless people go off to college and return home by the end of the first semester after failing in their classes. I was determined not to be one of them. I ended the semester with a 3.46 GPA (thanks for holding me to high standards Dad, because this wasn't my best), but I had begun to push physical boundaries, although I had yet to have sex. This was a perfect example of why you should always set audacious goals.

I did exactly what I set out to do: I didn't go home, and I didn't have sex. The problem is that those goals were extremely low. I didn't set out to do my absolute best in school, I just told myself I didn't want to go home. So I didn't. That 3.46 never impressed me because in one of my classes, I was being challenged by a great professor and I folded like origami—I got a C. When it came to sex, the bar was never high enough. The goal should have been purity instead of abstinence in one category.

Conviction and compromise cannot co-exist.

If the first semester was me not doing my best, then the second semester can only be described by one word: Failure. As tough as I was on myself for not setting high enough goals the first time around, this time, I had no goals at all. I went from a 3.46 GPA to a 0.8 GPA.

No, that's not a typo. In my second semester I had a 0.8 GPA.

I earned 4 Fs and 1 A.

How did I get one A?

There was a girl in whom I was interested in that class. I'm not sure who was using whom, but I agreed to help her with her work, if she would just let me use her book. I saved money and she got help from the smartest person in the class. A real win-win situation. Plus, there seemed to be a mutual attraction. Everything seemed to be going great—until it wasn't.

Eventually, we were chillin', and it came out that I wasn't having sex. She said that it was okay, but her body language said otherwise. We hung out a few times after that, but the vibe was off. The chemistry wasn't the same. Deep down I knew that it was a problem for her, and all of that came to a head on one particular day.

Every time I think of that day it's like a scene out of a movie. I lived in a different dorm than her, so I had to walk a good distance to see her. On the way it started raining—hard—and I got soaked. I was sitting on the very edge of the bed trying not to make a mess and I notice her on her phone a lot texting someone. Then after a few texts, a phone call. I could only hear half of the dialogue, but sometimes you gotta read between the lines. In between those lines was a message for me: "D'Andre, it's time to go!" Someone else was coming over, and I had a strong feeling they were not about to study.

Something happened to me that day. That was the day I began to head down a path of self-destruction. That was the day I decided that waiting wasn't worth it anymore. There were things that happened prior to this incident that contributed to this decision, but that was the straw that broke the camel's back.

Remove the Labels

On that day, I decided I was going to have sex!

As I walked home in the rain, these are the thoughts that filled my head:

Stupid! You look like a fool. You just got played, man!

Great self-talk, D'Andre.

All these women out here just want sex!

Really bro?! All of them, huh?! Or maybe it's just the ones you're talking to.

If that's the type of [dude] they want, then that's the type of [dude] they'll get!"

First of all, who is "they"? Secondly, instead of worrying about what type of dude they want, how about you worry about the type of man you want to become.

This was before I learned the strategy of personifying my negative thinking pattern and filtering my thoughts. When I think back on how I used to perceive and think about things, I am just in awe of how ignorant I was. But I didn't have the emotional maturity at the time.

If you've watched the documentary on that popular streaming platform (the one people use for date night when they really wanna "chill" with someone) about the Chicago Bulls, you'll notice that Michael Jordan took slights personally. He then used that as fuel for his competitive nature. After studying some of the greatest people in their given craft, I've learned that many of their celebrated attributes are actually signs of brokenness. Many of them point to someone who doubted them in the past and they use that as a source of motivation. Many of the G.O.A.T.S. (Greatest of All Time) in their given field are known as "super-competitive." The competitiveness is just a façade to cover a wound from their past that has yet to be healed. The wound is usually the same for them all: insecurity and inadequacy.

Isn't it ironic that the very thing that hurt these people the most is the same thing that made them great?

I personally know all about the hidden insecurity behind competitiveness. Growing up around sports and being a male there were only two types of people: winners and losers. I developed what I called a "competitive nature" because I never wanted to be labeled as a loser. This mentality spilled over into my life in a detrimental way.

The "winners vs. losers" mentality caused me to see life in a narrow-minded way. I began to see things as black and white and didn't leave much room for gray—or any other colors for that matter. This rigidity in my worldview was detrimental to my relationships. The smallest slight or perceived sign of disrespect and I'd cut a person off. I was the classic case of "leaving before getting left." Everything I did was about winning, reputation and protecting myself at all costs.

Well, after feeling humiliated and walking in the rain twice, I "took this personally." That day I felt like a loser. I left broken and with a chip on my shoulder. I never wanted to feel that way again, so I came up with a solution.

> No temptation has overtaken you that is not common to man. God is faithful, and he will not let you be tempted beyond your ability, but with the temptation he will also provide the way of escape, that you may be able to endure it. ~1 Corinthians 10:13

God is so good because he tried to save me from myself. That same night I set out to have sex, but God blocked it! Some unexpected obstacles got in my way. (Yeah, I'm not sharing that story. Ha-ha. Only a few know that one.) This was crucial. God was giving me the opportunity to think about this critical decision one last time. What did I do with this gracious gift from God? I set up another opportunity and did it anyway.

This is another example of why I was lame. After all of this time of waiting, I decided to make a life-altering decision about my life because of other people. I let their problems become mine. If that's what I wanted to do and that's who I wanted to be, it shouldn't have mattered what they thought of me.

The moment I lost my virginity I had an out of body experience. Instantly I felt the weight of my decision and felt regret. I knew I had let down God, myself and my future wife and family. I would rather have just done it because I had an urge or out of pure lust than for the reason I did. I had broken a promise I had made before God and to myself, and I did it for the wrong reasons.

Thank God for a praying grandmother!

Shoutout to my NaNa (nay-nuh)! I come from a family of ministers and saw people pray in church, but when I think of how I truly learned how to pray, it was from her. A day or so later, my aunt called me and straight-up asked me if I was still a virgin because NaNa had a feeling something was going on with me as it related to that. How did she know?! I hadn't been home in weeks. I hadn't posted ANYTHING about this. The Holy Spirit, that's how! I lied of course and denied the truth, but that didn't stop the spirit of conviction from working on me. Unfortunately, there was also an opposing force at work on my heart.

Satan.

And I heard a loud voice saying in heaven, Now is come salvation, and strength, and the kingdom of our God, and the power of his Christ: for **the accuser of our brethren** is cast down, which accused them before our God day and night.
Revelation 12:10

That's exactly who Satan is, the accuser of the brethren. And by brethren, I mean each and every one of us. He wants to use our past as a weapon against us. I always say that when sin is driving (or Satan for that matter), then guilt and shame are in the backseat. At this critical juncture, the enemy was beginning to infiltrate my mind with sin, shame, and guilt.

The first few days, I isolated myself. This is exactly what he (the enemy) wants you to do because "where two or three are gathered together **in my name**, I (God) am in the midst" (Matthew 18:20). Then, I replayed my decisions over and over and over in my mind, rehashing and reliving the guilt. After torturing my mind for days, in my ultimate moment of brokenness and weakness, he whispered this in my ear:

"You've already done it now, so what's the point of trying to stop. You've already messed up and there's nothing you can do about it"
-Satan, the biggest liar of them all!

Unfortunately in that season in my life, I chose to believe his lies. I continued down a sinful path of fornication and debauchery for a while after I bought that lie. Eventually, I began to come to my senses, but I was in shackles and chains due to my sin. By God's divine providence, a chance encounter would be a major turning point in my life.

Going into my sophomore year, I was humbled by my 0.8 GPA experience and I was grateful for God's grace in allowing me to stay enrolled at Texas Southern University. Although I had such a terrible GPA, I was never actually on academic probation because my other grades and early college GPA balanced out that bad semester. I did, however, lose some scholarships. But just to be in school was a blessing and I wanted to start prioritizing family. I decided I wanted to attend the annual TSU Labor Day Classic with all of my family. The problem was that it had sold out. Quick!

I was only able to purchase two tickets and I still needed about ten more. This is where God stepped into the situation.

Heading back to my dorm, I ran into this girl I had never met before and never saw again. I don't even think we told each other our names. Somehow the subject of the game came up and I asked her if she knew where I could get some more tickets. She gave me the number of someone selling them. I texted this person, and they told me to meet them in the student center. Come to find out it was a couple who were maybe in their mid- to late thirties. I bought the tickets and my family and I headed to the game. At the game, oddly enough, we ran into the couple and it turned out that the husband knew my grandparents. Then the unthinkable happened.

As it turned out, this man was over the Baptist Student Ministry at Texas Southern! My NaNa was in heaven. She had been telling me to join the BSM since before I had even stepped foot on campus. It's not that I wasn't interested, as the above text of this chapter illustrates, it just wasn't high on my priority list at the time. So, I joined the BSM, turned my life around, and everyone lived happily ever after! Right?!

Not so fast!

Sin never wants you to leave, and it's not going anywhere without a fight! Although I wanted to change, my flesh was comfortable with where I was. At this point, I still didn't have a vehicle, so a few times I reached out for a ride to the Bible study. Every time I reached out, I kid you not, I would back out 30 minutes prior. This went on for several months until I finally decided it was time for a change.

I had this war waging inside of me. A part of me yearned to be in fellowship with other believers and to be in church again, but the shame was just too much. I know this sounds silly, but

> I felt like I had a sin shirt on.

I believed that when I walked in a room, I had this invisible shirt on with all of my sins written on it as if it were a design. I'd run into the leader of the BSM several times and he would always smile and speak to me, and I would instantly feel convicted because I knew I should be going to his Bible studies. He never tried to beat me over the head with the Bible or make me feel bad—my own personal conviction was enough. Finally, one day I decided I was going to ignore those lies from the devil in my head about my past. What I had already done was not a lie, but the notion that I had to stay in that place for the rest of my life was not true—at all! That one decision on that particular day to attend that first Bible study changed my life forever.

I ended up joining the Baptist Student Ministry at Texas Southern and even became the president during my last two years of college. I went on my first-ever plane ride on a mission trip to Jamaica. I accepted my calling as a minister of the gospel because of that trip and grew in my faith. It all started when I began to realize my true identity in Christ.

The things I have already shared and will continue to share as you read the rest of this book may be entertaining, but that's not the purpose. I'm not "clout-chasing" either and doing this for some likes and social media relevance. I do want to be an Amazon best-selling author. I do aspire to be a New York Times best-selling author more than once in my lifetime, but at the core of why I am doing this is one thing: to help other people like me. That means this book is for everyone because we all have pain and we all have a purpose. In addition, everyone has had an identity crisis at some point in their lives, and if you haven't yet, you more than likely will.

Your worth doesn't have to be proven!

Jesus did that on the cross!

Prior to my current career, I worked at a few department stores as a cashier and as an overnight stocker. Loss prevention was always a focus in both positions. The word we heard the most was *shrinkage*. In black culture this means the loss of hair length after your hair dries. It's a good sign of healthy hair! However, in department store lingo this means damaged or stolen merchandise. One of the ways we prevented shrinkage as overnight stockers was to secure the price tag to the item with a security tag. There are two types of tags. One of the tags will disperse ink if it is improperly removed and the other will make a sound if it is taken past the store's entrance. Even with all of these preventative measures, there were still other ways people would try and beat the system.

One of the most common methods was for people to move the item to a clearance section and switch the tags with a similar lower priced item. Other times, people would just rip off the tag and hope to just negotiate a price. Most customers didn't realize that our computer system has a registry of items with prices, but there were items that even the computers couldn't locate a price for. We still had one more trick up our sleeves. As a stocker, after we placed the security tag on a shoe, or any item with a hard surface, the next thing we were supposed to do before taking it out to the floor was to put the price on the bottom of the item in permanent ink. This ensured that no matter where the item was taken in the store, no matter if the tag was taken off, no matter what kind of label people tried to put on it, it always retained its true value.

If I were in a church right now, somebody would yell out, "Preach!"

Then, I would respond by saying, "I already am!"

I believe we've all been that pair of shoes in the department store. Sin has taken us to some places that tarnished us. We've been stripped of things due to the calamities of life. People have even tried to put their own labels on us:

Fat.

Dumb.

Ugly.

Ghetto.

Corny.

Lame.

Slut.

And the list goes on. But, no matter how far sin has taken you away, no matter what your bad decisions have robbed you of, and no matter what labels people have tried to place on you,

> Jesus marked your value permanently when He died on the cross for your sins:

You are priceless!

Just like the shoes, you have a designer and He assigned a value to you the moment He created you. It doesn't matter where you're from or where you grew up. Your past behavior does not define you! The things people have called you are irrelevant to your true identity.

I want you to find a mirror or even turn your phone to selfie mode and say the following aloud to yourself:

"I am forgiven!" (John 1:9)

"I am wonderfully made!" (Psalm 139:14)

"God loves me in spite of my flaws!" (John 3:16)

Remove the Labels

There are countless other verses that point to who you really are in God's eyes. There isn't enough room or time to share them all, but the point of me sharing them is this:

I finally decided that if I am going to be loved, rejected, or accepted I am going to do so being my real, authentic self. Take it or leave it! I refuse to waste any more time trying to be the person I think people want me to be or basing my self-worth on their approval.

I want to challenge you to do two things:

Find out who you truly are.

Be that person in every situation.

You are a person of value and you offer something the world needs.

Be you.

That's more than enough.

PART II
THE ASHES

After phoenix is consumed by the fire, all that remains are the ashes...

Chapter 4

HOLD ON TO YOUR HOPE

"I wake up in the morning and I ask myself

Is life worth living? Should I blast myself?"

-"Changes" by Tupac Shakur feat. Talent

"I can't breathe!"

They weren't trying to be famous.

They weren't trying to become the faces of a movement.

Men like Eric Garner, George Floyd and over 70 others killed in police custody after uttering those three words, were just trying to breathe—literally. They just wanted to live. They had families and loved ones and were hoping they'd get the chance to see them again. Unfortunately, they were robbed of that opportunity unjustly. Although I have never been physically assaulted in the custody of police—or even arrested for that matter—I can see a lot of myself in these men, and I can relate to them.

For starters, I am a black man.

And being Black or a person of color comes with a weight and set of obstacles and barriers that can sometimes seem insurmountable. As I stated earlier, I whole-heartedly believe that race is socially constructed, but that doesn't change the fact that I deal with race every day I step out the door. I once had a white co-worker tell me it was all in my head. She believed the fears I have as a black man and the impact they have on me were just figments of my imagination. I can only control my actions. I can only control the way I see the world. No matter what I do, I cannot change the way I am perceived by others. That is their choice to make.

"It is impossible to be unarmed when our blackness is the weapon they fear."

The reason I can relate to those men is because I could easily have been one of them. Any time I pass a cop, my heart begins to race. If I happen to get pulled over it's even worse. Simple activities such as just going for a jog in my neighborhood are now cause for concern. When I am walking or out for a run, thoughts of Ahmaud Arbery are in my mind: another unarmed Black who was killed for simply jogging in his neighborhood.

Those three words, "I can't breathe," were impacting my life years before the unjust deaths of these men. Before this phrase became a rally cry and a movement, they were my daily reality. Although I have never been clinically diagnosed, I believe for years I have suffered from anxiety.

I don't know exactly when it happened, but anxiety became a part of my everyday life. Remember when I said fear became the lens through which I filtered everything in life? Well, being constantly anxious was a by-product of this fear.

Eventually, anxiety not only consumed me, but it controlled me.

My first encounter with anxiety was not my own but witnessing someone else deal with it. When I began middle school, I really started to get into football. One of the players I was a fan of was Ricky Williams. He was a former Heisman Trophy winner from the University of Texas, the 2002 NFL rushing yards leader, an All-Pro and Pro-Bowl selection, plus he had dreads. I always thought they were cool, as a kid. But he had a very odd habit:

He would conduct interviews in his helmet—a helmet that was equipped with a tinted visor.

"Well isn't it normal for a football player to have his helmet on in an interview?" No! This was not normal! I would later discover that he suffered from an extreme case of social anxiety. He would use the helmet and the visor as a way of coping with the anxiety brought on by the reporters and the media. The more I think about it, what he did isn't so odd because I see people do it every day.

No, I don't see people walking around with football helmets on their heads, but I do see people using strange methods to deal with their feelings of anxiousness:

People wearing headphones with no music playing

Kids wearing hoodies in 90° + temperatures

People scrolling on their phone pretending to read something just to avoid interacting with people

If I'm keeping it a hunnit (being honest), I thought what Ricky Williams was doing was funny or some sort of joke. In my naivety, I couldn't fathom the concept of social anxiety at the time. I couldn't comprehend how someone could be a millionaire, a professional athlete, rich and famous, and not be able to handle being questioned by the media. I didn't understand what he was dealing with until it happened to me.

"Remember, when you point a finger at someone, there are three more pointing back at you."

Just like Ricky, I've dealt with an extreme case of social anxiety. When I was around people in most settings, I would be fine. In fact, I'd probably be the most talkative person in the room, but something strange would happen when I was in larger crowds. First, my breathing would start to become heavy and labored. Next, my heart would begin to race and thump out of my chest. The last thing that was altered was my gait. Every step I took felt like I had cinder blocks strapped to the bottom of my feet. If you've never experienced this, what I am going to say next may seem strange:

I felt like everyone around me was looking at me and making judgments about me.

The irony about this is that, deep down, I knew this was absolutely false. Logically, I could see with my own eyes that everyone was engaged in whatever it was they were doing, so they weren't even thinking about me. On a deeper level, I knew it just didn't make sense.

"Fear is a damn lie!!!"- Christina D. Sanders@thepolichic

I'll never forget the day Professor Tunechi (we called her that because of her affinity for Lil Wayne) said that, and I agree with her. While the source of our fear is usually from a real experience, the magnitude of the fear and the extent in which we allow the fear to dictate our lives is usually a false narrative we create in our own minds. When I would find myself in crowds, I knew that what my anxiety was telling me was a lie, but the changes in my body and the emotions I felt were real. Isn't it ironic how something we imagine—that may not ever happen—can cause changes in our body and present reality? I wish my anxiety stopped at the social level, but that was only the beginning.

Fear is pervasive. If you allow it to occupy space in your mind, body or spirit, it seeks to spread and multiply itself and its influence. Anxiety became such a normal part of my life; I didn't even bother to rectify it. Without realizing it, I literally built my life around my anxiousness.

When experiencing something unpleasant, what is our natural response?

Avoidance.

I was the master of avoidance. Anything and everything that caused me to feel uncomfortable, I avoided.

Making eye contact with people? No way! Just walk with your head down.

Trying something new? Nah! You might embarrass yourself, so just keep doing what you know.

What I did to avoid large crowds is embarrassing to say the least. If I had to walk somewhere and got caught off guard by a large crowd, I would change my path just to avoid the feeling of anxiousness they caused me.

Is that really that embarrassing, D'Andre?

Is that really a big deal?

It is when you're 90% of the way to your destination and nearly make yourself or actually cause yourself to be late just to avoid a temporary moment of discomfort. That is when I started to realize that I had a major problem.

We all deal with anxiety on some level. Yours may not be as extreme as mine, or it could be worse. I used to think what Ricky Williams did was laughable until I dealt with it myself and could understand him better. Someone may read my story about my fear of crowds and laugh, but we should never belittle or judge someone else's fear. I enjoy public speaking, but I know it is one of the top fears in the world. We all fear something that someone else doesn't and vice versa. Instead of using this as an opportunity to judge or demean someone, let it be the perfect opportunity for us to help someone overcome their fear and bring them comfort in their struggle. At some point in our lives, we will find ourselves on both sides of fear.

The question is, how do I know if my anxiety is a "big deal"?

We all deal with anxiety from time to time, but when it begins to dictate your life is when it's a problem. Do you find yourself checking in with anxiety before making a decision? Is it causing you to miss out on things that are important to you? Growth happens when we are uncomfortable, and anxiety is the epitome of comfort-seeking. Anxiety draws invisible boundaries in our lives and keeps us boxed in. It causes us to be risk-averse and miss out on being the best version of ourselves and reaching our fullest potential.

Not only did my anxiety almost rob me of my potential, it nearly robbed me of my life. I was so ravaged by anxiety that it caused me to become severely depressed. I was depressed so long that I was essentially hopeless. My mind would race about thoughts of the future, wondering if things would ever change for the better in my life or if they would remain the same. Eventually, this led me to a dark place.

Fortunately, I never attempted suicide. How? I don't know. I did think about death frequently during that time. It's not even so much that I wanted to die, it just seemed like living was too hard. Death seemed like an escape from what felt like insurmountable circumstances to me at the time.

At the core of every negative emotion is a degree of selfishness. I am not saying that it's wrong to feel anger, or sadness, or to be depressed, but these negative emotions are allowed to fester when we become consumed with ourselves. I won't speak for you, but I know this was the case for myself. I was so consumed by the negative emotions plaguing my mind that I couldn't see anything else outside of how I felt. This severe grade of depression was not something that was just an issue in my adolescence, it followed me into adulthood.

So, how did I overcome it?

I had to find something bigger than myself in which to place my hope. I had to find a source of inspiration that could sustain me in times of adversity and conflict. It's apparent that I am a believer, so ultimately my hope is in Christ, but at the time my relationship with God had not reached the maturity that it is at today. I was literally just looking for a reason to get out of the bed each day.

I stopped living for myself. I started thinking about the people I loved.

My sisters.

My brother.

My cousins.

What would it say to them if I gave up? What kind of example would I be setting? With that on my mind and heart I began to use that as a driving force for everything I did. When I would get ready to give up or quit, I would think of a relative whom I didn't want to let down. Thinking of them began to give me hope.

Over the years, I have come to realize that hope is necessary if we are going to persevere in life. You can have everything, but without hope, you'll feel like you have nothing. On the contrary you could literally have absolutely nothing, but if you have hope, you have everything.

Maybe you're facing a difficult situation in your life right now. A health scare. Job loss. Family crisis. Maybe the thought of what's at stake is giving you anxiety, causing stress or leading you into a state of depression. You have to hold onto your hope. Find something to believe in, even when it's not yourself at the time.

Say this, "It won't always be like this!"

You may feel like you are never going to make it out of this situation, but it won't last forever. Hold onto your hope!

Hold On to Your Hope

Chapter 5

MOURN YOUR INNOCENCE

"I seen the innocence leave your eyes.
I still mourn this death." - Jay Z

Death is a part of life.

Kind of oxymoronic isn't it?

I have come to learn that the more vivid a memory is, the deeper the emotion attached to it. Death and life may be on opposite ends of the spectrum, but both have the same emotional potency.

Nothing can be compared to the love parents feel when they first lay eyes upon the beauty that is their newborn child. There is no combination of words to describe the euphoria engulfing them as they hold their baby in their arms.

Death is similar in the experience it creates.

There is no combination of words that can console someone who has endured the loss of a loved one. Whether one has lost a pet, friend, relative, parent or child, nothing can truly comfort the bereaved. Time may allow the sting of death to lessen, but it never leaves completely. You will always remember exactly where you were when you got the news.

I know this from personal experience.

I was in third grade at the time and got off of my bus like I would any other day. As I walked into the house, I instantly knew that something was off. Both of my parents were home in the afternoon and not in their work clothes. Some people call it "energy" and others say it's "vibes," but I knew something bad had just happened. My parents' countenance was somber and melancholy as they said, "D'Andre, we have something to tell you: Granny Brown passed away this afternoon."

"No she didn't! Stop playing!" I said in disbelief. How could she have died? I had just gone to visit her in the hospital the night before, and she seemed to be doing better. After denying it once more and questioning their sincerity, it finally dawned on me:

She was really dead.

I had been to funerals before, but this was the first time I had experienced the death of someone I was really close to and cared about. Once I allowed myself to accept the harsh reality that my maternal grandmother was no longer with us, a rush of tears began to flow from my eyes. My mother came to comfort me as we cried together.

Death can unite us all because it is inevitable in each and every one of our lives. At some point in our existence we will witness it and eventually experience it. There is one death that we all must grieve at some point in our lives. Many of us are still mourning its loss as of today.

> When did you experience the death of your innocence?

I was around 10 years old.

One thing I give my parents credit for is striving to keep me sheltered. They did their best to monitor the things I watched on television, the music I listened to, and censored the topics I was exposed to in conversations. Throughout my formative years, I had a consistent bedtime: 8:00 pm. I was never allowed to spend the night with anyone who was not a family member. But no matter how much a parent tries, eventually a child will encounter the world for themselves and will be faced with its perils.

This is the day I will never forget. The day some of my peers exposed me to pornography.

In an attempt to remove my childhood label of snitch, I took a vow of secrecy. Well that is, until the bill came in the mail and the truth was exposed. The adults addressed the situation and consequences were handed out, but nothing could allow what was seen to be erased from my mind. A seed was planted in my mind, and for years it lay dormant, but eventually it would grow into a truly ugly weed in the garden of my soul.

The question remains:

When did you witness the death of your innocence?

For some, it was frequently witnessing domestic violence in their home. Others may have not only witnessed the violence but may have been on the receiving end of it themselves. Countless children are stripped of their innocence at the hands of a molester. For others, the loss of their innocence is not as physically harmful, but just as damaging psychologically.

For many kids, they are robbed of their childhood simply by having to grow up too fast. In their formative years, they were given the daunting task of being a babysitter, a cook, a tutor and, in some ways, a parent to younger siblings while having to learn how to role switch between being a child and adult in any given situation. Maybe you were a teen who was counted upon to contribute to the household financially and still go to school during the day. I could go on and on with different scenarios and examples of this, but I believe you get the point.

No matter your background, eventually your innocence is taken from you one way or another. As we emerge into adulthood from adolescence, society teaches us how to put on façades, and many of us are simply wearing masks in order to hide the painful wounds of our childhood. There may be scars left by the trauma you endured, but there are two ways you can look at it:

You can view them as painful reminders of the past; or You can see them as evidence of healing and survival.

How you choose to perceive your past is critical to your ability to move forward in life.

For many of us, the second option is the road less traveled—we choose to bury our pain.

When the trauma is too much to process, we take the shovel of shame, excavate a hole in the depths of our souls, and cover our painful past with the debris of regret, fear, bitterness, pride, and other materials that amount to a pile of dirt.

The paradox of this approach is that no matter how much we try to fill the hole created by the pain of our past, no matter how many different things we attempt to cover the hollow created in our childhood, we are still left feeling empty.

What if I told you there is a better way? A different way to deal with our traumatic experiences.

There are two reasons why we bury something:

We want to hide it.

We are putting it to rest.

It is time for you to lay your innocence to rest. A wise person once said,

> "Live your life in such a way that the preacher doesn't have to lie at your funeral."

I have been to many funerals in my lifetime and you can always tell what type of person they were based on the way people interact at the service and what people say about the deceased.

The good news is that you are in charge of this funeral service. You do not have to lie about anything. You can tell the truth—and the truth shall set you free.

I encourage you not to bury your pain by hiding it, but rather to bury it in the sense of putting it to rest, i.e., a funeral service for your innocence. The pain, the trauma, abuse or neglect you may have endured as a child is going to continue to affect you until you begin the process of restoration. The first part of that process is to unpack all of the pain and actually allow yourself to feel it. The sooner you feel, the sooner you can truly heal.

Say this, "I will no longer suppress any trauma or negative emotions from my past. I will give myself the space to unpack these emotions so I can process them fully."

Chapter 6

ADDRESS THE ADDICTIONS

I think the currency of leadership is transparency.
-Howard Schultz

Hello, my name is D'Andre Lacy, and I am a recovering pornography addict.

Whether you know me personally or this is your first encounter, you can never look at me the same after reading such a statement. In the words of Brené Brown, I am sure I'll have a "vulnerability hangover" (when we experience regret about expressing ourselves and begin to agonize over how it is going to be perceived) after revealing such a personal part of my story. But why?! Why share such an embarrassing thing about myself? Why unnecessarily endure the possible ridicule, judgment, and criticism that could come from uncovering this secret sin?

Freedom! That's why!

"Vulnerability is our most accurate measure of courage."
- Dr. Brené Brown

I would be lying if I were to say I'm not afraid. I could put on the façade of being cool, calm, and collected, but I've decided to take the huge risk of unveiling this secret. In the face of my fears, shame and regret—I look beyond its paralyzing mirage and see a hopeful future. I see people of all nations, ages, ethnicities, and backgrounds plagued by this issue freed from its bondage and walking in liberty—and that is worth it all.

Don't be misled—you cannot mock the justice of God. You will always harvest what you plant. Those who live only to satisfy their own sinful nature will harvest decay and death from that sinful nature. But those who live to please the Spirit will harvest everlasting life from the Spirit. (Galatians 6:7-8)

When my innocence was robbed of me, a seed was planted. Anyone who knows anything about gardening knows that the results are not immediate. Although for a couple of years, nothing seemed to come of that day, beneath the surface a seed of destruction lay dormant, taking root in the soil of my soul. Eventually, the day would come when it began to bear fruit.

I hope and pray that you have received your salvation, but that is not the point behind me sharing that quote. The point I'm making is that no addict ever intended to become one. Ravi Zaccharias said, "Sin will take you farther than you want to go, keep you longer than you want to stay, and cost you more than you want to pay." Any moment we live our life without intentionality, we create an environment conducive for negative consequences. We can either lead our heart or be led by it.

Many of you have heard the definition of insanity: doing the same thing and expecting a different result. Let me introduce you to its sibling: addiction. Addiction has a connotation of drug and substance abuse, but it is not limited to just those things alone. An addiction is doing anything harmful for a temporary relief or satisfaction it provides. This is why I can say with all honesty that I am a recovering addict:

Pornography became my secret addiction.

A gateway drugs is a "habit-forming drug that, while itself not addictive, may lead to the use of other addictive drugs." When your brain is exposed to certain substances, they can boost dopamine levels. Repeated exposure to such a substance over time eventually causes your body to produce less dopamine. Eventually harder substances are sought to produce the effect or "high" that the original substance once produced. This, my friend, is how an addiction gets started.

My venture into the snares of porn is not solely the fault of the peers who first exposed me to it:

I played a part in my own demise.

And once innocence is gone, it can never return. However, purity is something that can always be pursued. I have a strong passion for protecting the innocence and purity of children due to my own early exposure and bad decision making that destroyed my innocence and purity as a youth.

What began as curiosity, ended in destruction. Yes, it is true that my peers exposed my mind to sex through conversations, pornography, and personal tales of their own experiences, I am not a total victim in this situation. Although my sheltered, young mind could not fully comprehend what I was being told or shown, I always knew it was wrong. No, it was not wrong to be curious, nor was it wrong to want to know more about the subject, but even at that age I knew pornography and certain films and shows were not the proper channels for educating myself.

I am not yet a parent myself, but I have a word of advice for any parents out there: Do not be passive about the issues that matter.

Address the Addictions

Let me also begin by saying that I'm not throwing my family, guardians, or mentors under the bus. I am not blaming them for all of my bad decisions in this area, but I do wish they would have talked to me about it sooner, more frequently, and in more detail. I believe by the time they thought I needed to know; society had already begun to influence me on the subject.

> "You do not control your future, your habits do!"
> -Dr. Myles Munroe

In sixth grade, a classmate once asked me, "Do you masturbate? My brother does and I was just wondering if all boys do that." I looked at her with such a blank look on my face—not out of disgust or shame, but because I had never heard the term before. I said, "Masturbation?! What is that?" She began to explain to me what it was and afterwards, I told her that I really didn't do it. She laughed and said she did not believe me. "All boys do!", she said. Unbeknownst to me, later on that year, I would begin to do it myself and thus make her theory seem more like a fact. This was the beginning of a destructive habit that would haunt me for many years to come.

Sin, just like addiction, has a progressive nature. Just watching the racy films, wasn't enough. Then, masturbation in addition to these films, just didn't quite do it for me. I needed more dopamine! I honestly cannot pinpoint the day it happened, but eventually I began the habit of consuming pornography.

This dirty little secret of mine eventually became a crutch. I began to become more and more dependent upon the momentary high I felt when consuming this content. Eventually, it became a coping mechanism—for everything: sadness, loneliness, rejection, stress, and any and every negative emotion in between.

Pornography and masturbation became a way for me to cope with the harsh realities of life.

My struggle with this addiction has taught me many things with one of them being to refrain from judging others. Growing up, I was always confounded by people who couldn't stop smoking or drinking or gambling. I would often ask myself. "If you knew it could hurt you or put your family in jeopardy, then why do it?!" The naivety and self-righteousness of my younger self could not comprehend the depth of the struggle that addiction manifests. Little did I know at the time of these thoughts that I too would one day walk many miles in their shoes.

One of my favorite high school teachers (my economics teacher to be exact) taught me an acronym I will never forget:

TINSTAAFL: There Is No Such Thing As A Free Lunch

Everything costs you something.

This deviant behavior had a hefty price tag. My habit cost me countless hours of time, endless amounts of dignity, unmeasurable shame, and hindered my walk with God. I boldly share this in the hope that it will lead to the liberation of countless others who are caught in its clutches. Sidenote: this issue is also much more prevalent in women than people realize. The poster child of porn is a pubescent teenage boy, but that is not the only demographic struggling with this. Before you tune my message out and assume this doesn't apply to you, realize this is bigger than porn, sex or even drug use. Addiction and its many forms are just a by-product of the real issue: self-medication.

What is your "drug" of choice?

You can never judge a book by its cover. Unfortunately for me, my self-medicating did not just end with porn—I also had another less visible issue. I used food to bring me comfort.

Address the Addictions

If you saw my slender, lanky build in person you would be none the wiser. We automatically infer that only people of a portly build struggle with food, but outward appearance does not equate to issues with food on either side of the spectrum.

I allowed food to become a buffer between myself and my emotions. Instead of growing through experiencing my feelings and learning from them, I sought ways to dull and desensitize myself from the discomfort they caused. Bored? Eat. Lonely? Eat. Sad? Eat. Stressed about a test (that I probably did not adequately study for)? Grab some of my favorite snacks to ease the tension. My freshman year of college I had an entire post-test snack lineup.

This is how it went: First, I would procrastinate and not study the way I should (partially due to depression and also because I literally did not learn how to study until college and beyond). Next, the week of the test would come, and I would promise myself to buckle down—but you guessed it— I didn't! Then, TEST DAY! You know you haven't studied when every answer sounds right—or wrong—and then you look back on your Scantron sheet and it seems like you bubbled too many A's or C's. Now, you're erasing and attempting to evenly distribute the amount of each letter on your answer sheet. My favorite part of the test was when I turned it in because I would always think to myself, *At least it's over now! It's out of my control at this point.* The momentary relief was always premature because my mind would now be consumed by the outcome of the test and my overwhelming shame and regret at my lack of preparation. In the words of T.I., I had to alleviate this anxiety—"expeditiously."

I walked to the neighborhood corner store to purchase my go-to comfort snacks:

1 bag of sour apple rings

1 bag of peach rings

(They were two for a dollar—so I had to.)

A Snickers ice cream bar

Arizona tea

1-2 pints of ice cream

(Depending on how bad it was that day)

It gets worse. I am embarrassed to say it, but I had an entire system and plan to console my agony from start to finish. The ice cream bar was my "walking back to the dorm snack." Then, I would eat one of the bags of candy. Depending upon the day, I may even gulp down the drink. I always saved the ice cream for when I made it back to my dorm. Its flavor brought comfort and consolation with each and every bite—or so I thought. I was merely attempting to numb the pain that I had brought upon myself.

Pain is not our enemy; pain is our friend. Pain is an indicator that something we did or are doing is wrong. When we make a conscious effort to ignore it, we are committing ourselves to an even greater affliction in the future.

I like to think of pain as a check-engine light. If you have ever been in a car, there are different lights on the dashboard. These lights all are connected to different parts of the engine and other components of the vehicle. They light up only when there is something malfunctioning or broken in the car. I know people who drive around with the light on and just ignore it. Some of them say they do not have the time nor the money to deal with it, so they just continue to drive as if nothing is wrong. There are a few problems with this:

Just because you ignore the light, it does not change the fact that something is broken or malfunctioning.

Many parts in a vehicle are interconnected so ignoring it can lead to other components being damaged. Whatever you couldn't afford to do before is only going to be more costly the longer you wait.

Ignoring the indicator lights on your vehicle is not only harmful to your wallet, but it could possibly put your life and the lives of your passengers and other people on the road in jeopardy. There are other lights on the dashboard for things such as fuel, oil, and air bags amongst other things, but the check-engine light is not just for one area, it is connected to multiple areas within the vehicle. Someone who drives with it on all the time becomes desensitized to the problem they were once aware of, and ignorant of the new issues caused by the original problem due to their refusal to fully acknowledge it.

The use of food not only didn't alleviate my problems, it added to my list of issues. The best thing it did was provide a temporary relief to difficult situations in life in the form of a distraction. But, when the fleeting moment of relief ended, I had new problems to deal with in addition to the old ones I was attempting to run from. I never had cavities, until college (probably due to my newfound freedom and lack of constraint when it came to food). I gained over 20 pounds my first year of school and did not lose the weight until years later. The constant diet filled with excessive sodium, sugar, processed foods, and excessive empty calories was like a ticking time bomb for my health. If my body was a vehicle, I was ignoring all of the indicator lights.

No matter how much I ate, I was never satisfied. I thought I wanted more food, but deep down inside, I knew it would never be enough. When I finished eating, no matter how close to capacity my stomach was, I still felt an emptiness. There was a void created in my soul by years of self-esteem issues, depression, procrastination, and underachievement. The peace I tried to find on my plate could only be realized in my purpose. The "fullness" I wanted to feel in my belly was really a desire for fulfillment in my life.

Are you ready to address your addictions?

I have heard that giving babies a bottle every time they cry, teaches them to use food as a method of coping instead of learning how to self-soothe. Your parents might have taken you shopping every time you were sad or disappointed about something. Growing up, a parent or loved one may have used alcohol to celebrate, when they were depressed or even angry and now you do the same. When we shield our loved ones from feeling their emotions in their formative and adolescent years, it robs them of the opportunity to develop their emotional intelligence. Maybe someone modeled or formed some of these habits in you when you were younger with good intentions, but now you are paying the price for their decisions as an adult.

We all have some area in our life in which we have formed unhealthy coping mechanisms. The day is today, and the time is now to draw the line in the sand and say, "Enough is enough!" The road is not going to be easy! It's going to take many moments of self-reflection, introspection and honesty. You're going to have to ask and answer some tough questions. But you don't need to relinquish the direction and purpose of your life over to an addiction. The truth is this:

You can't heal what you never reveal"

-Sean Carter

Again, I ask the same question once again:

What is your drug of choice?

Is it pornography?

Using food to comfort you?

Retail therapy?

(By the way, this is not a problem reserved for women because I know many guys with a huge collection of shoes).

Or something else?

We all find unhealthy ways to cope because we were not equipped with the tools to handle whatever the trigger emotion is that causes us to find solace in our unhealthy habit. The first step in overcoming is to realize you are not some weirdo or freak. You are not alone. The next step involves a moment of self-reflection.

In the same economics class from high school, we learned the term "opportunity cost." In a financial context, opportunity cost is the profit lost when one alternative is selected over another. For example, let's imagine there was a stock that has five-year returns of 5%. You decide to take $1,000 and invest in it rather than a stock that had five-year returns of 7%. The opportunity cost was the difference between what you chose and the next best alternative which would be 2%. In the context of life, opportunity cost has the same basic idea, but it can be applied to any choice we make. Essentially, we give up the next best alternative choice any and every time we make a decision.

What is your addiction costing you?

Now before you get holier-than-thou on me, I want you to pause for a moment of self-reflection in order to identify at least one.

It could be a behavior.

It could be a relationship.

It could even be social media.

The core component of an addiction is when a person is participating in something they know is not in their best interests, but just cannot seem to rid themselves of whatever it is. Really dig deep and bring this thing to your mind.

Do not continue reading until you find your addiction—most of us have one.

Now when you have it in mind, I want you to think about what it is costing you.

How much time do you waste on this behavior?

Does your coping mechanism cost you money?

How does it impact your relationships? If you were to continue engaging with it, where will you end up five years from now? Ten years?

Would you like the person you ended up becoming?

The first step to overcoming a problem is to admit that you have one:

My name is D'Andre Lacy and I am a recovering porn addict. I used to turn to food as a way of coping with my problems.

Now it's your turn.

My name is _____ and I struggle with _____.

Part III

THE REBIRTH

"There's still beauty when the ashes remain/You'll rise like a phoenix when it manifests its change" -@DJLinspires

Out of the ashes, the phoenix rises again!

Chapter 7

TAKE OWNERSHIP

"Most people would learn from their mistakes if they
weren't so busy denying them."
- Harold J. Smith

What are you waiting for?

An apology?

Validation from others?

Or maybe "it's just not the right time yet."

If you're anticipating an apology, just know it may never
come. When you find yourself seeking validation from
others, no matter how much they give you, it is never
enough!

The notion of "the perfect time" is mythical.

There is never going to be the right time to end a
relationship. That dream job you want is not just going to

fall into your lap. The weight you gained through emotional eating is not going to lose itself. That debt you got yourself into is not going to just disappear.

The perfect and only time to make the change you are seeking in your life is right now! Peace can only be found being present in the present moment. When we are experiencing anxiety, it is often because we are simultaneously worried about the past and the future. It is our mind's way of attempting to protect us from a pain that we have already experienced, by using the past as a reference point to predict what **may** happen in the future so we can avoid it happening again.

One of my favorite quotes is "90% of the things you worry about never happen." But if we allow ourselves to procrastinate due to our unchecked thought patterns, we just end up wasting time and eventually wasting our life. Tomorrow is never promised.

I was and still am a huge Kobe Bryant fan. Sadly, he is no longer with us. Rest in peace, Kobe. I know as an athlete and as a person, he was a polarizing figure, so if he is not someone whom you admire, that is fine. Regardless, we all can still learn from his life.

The most obvious glaring lesson is that death is something we will all face at the end of our lives. The catch is that none of us know when or under what circumstance we will experience it. What made his death so painful for me and many others, even if he was not your favorite basketball player, was that it was just so unexpected. He was a highly acclaimed athlete who had just recently retired. He had accomplished so much on the court and was starting to do just as much off the court. Many people were waiting with anticipation of what would be coming next—not only his life, but also the life of his daughter, Gianna.

There are so many stories about his legendary work ethic, but one stands out to me in particular. This story is from 2012 when Kobe was a member of the United States Men's National Basketball Team as they were preparing for the Olympics. A trainer came into contact with Kobe and they exchanged numbers. The trainer told him to reach out if he ever needed to do some extra conditioning, and he was in for a huge surprise.

A few days passed and Kobe finally reached out—at 4:15 am. Place yourself in the athletic trainer's shoes for a moment. How many of us would have missed the call let alone actually gotten up to meet him in order to train that early? Some opportunities are once-in-a-lifetime, and knowing this, the trainer did go meet him and worked out with him for over an hour.

When they finished, the trainer returned to his hotel room to get some rest for that day's practice at 11 am. When practice finally rolled around, the trainer noticed something peculiar as the players began to arrive. Kobe was alone on the other side of the court shooting jump shots drenched in sweat.

Rob (the trainer) walked over and asked Kobe what time he finished his workout. Kobe responded by saying, "Oh, just now. I wanted 800 makes so yeah, just now." Essentially Kobe Bryant arrived 7 hours earlier than he was supposed to and then proceeded to go through the actual practice that Team USA held that same day.

"I didn't feel good about myself if I wasn't doing everything I could to become the best version of myself. If I felt like I left anything on the table...ummm it would eat away at me—I wouldn't be able to look at myself in the mirror. So the reason why I can retire now and be completely comfortable about it is because I know I've done EVERYTHING I could to be the best basketball player I could be."
-Kobe Bryant

Take Ownership

As sad as it was to see KOBE pass at such a young age, it also was very inspiring. From what I learned about him from a distance, he lived each day as if it were his last. When it came to his preparation, he left no stone unturned. He went to extreme lengths to perfect his craft and become the best at whatever it was he did—even outside of basketball.

Many people were shocked at his death and saddened by all the things Kobe would not get to do as a result, but there is also a different way of looking at it too. I am in awe of all that he accomplished by the age of 41 years old:

Five-time NBA Champion

Two NBA Finals MVPs

Two-time Olympic Gold Medalist ('08, '12)

An Oscar in 2018 for the best animated short for *Dear Basketball*

As much as I enjoyed watching his basketball exploits, I believe I was most inspired by his Oscar award. In interviews after he retired, he often discussed how people doubted how serious he was about becoming a storyteller. His being honored with that award demonstrated the ability for anyone to reinvent themselves and to evolve at any stage in their life if they so desire. I believe his success manifested from his own belief in himself and that he was not waiting around for someone else's validation.

It may not be your fault, but it is your responsibility.

As we have already discussed, countless things happen in our lives that are out of our control. We did not choose our parents. We had no say in the type of family into which we were born. The way others perceive us and the judgment they pass on us is not for us to worry about. When things happen to us and people mistreat us, we have two options:

React

or

Respond

Your story may be filled with adversity and calamity at every turn. There may have been many terrible things that happened to you and situations you were forced to be in that were out of your control, but the one thing you always have control of is, whether or not you react or respond. So, whether you were born into poverty, molested, abused or suffered a gut-wrenching loss in your life, you get to choose.

Another important point is that although the words *react* and *respond* seem similar, the difference is that when you react, it is based in emotions, but when you respond, you are pulling from a place of reasoning and logic. A proper response requires mindfulness and reacting is the antithesis of being mindful.

Every single day of your life you are writing your story, and ultimately your obituary. It is imperative to approach everything you do in life with that end in mind. It is often said that when someone reaches the end of their life, they are much more likely to regret what they did not do than what they did.

Say this, "I am not waiting for someone to save me. I will not live my life with regret. I am taking action to build the life I want to live."

Take Ownership

Chapter 8

CHALLENGE THE B.S.

"Your actions will always follow your beliefs."
- David Childers (Facing the Giants)

Are you really gonna accept that b.s. in your life?

Taking ownership is about accepting responsibility and no longer seeing yourself as a victim. Yes, people have lied to you, labeled you, and left you, but that was out of your control. The only person you ever truly have authority over is yourself, and it's time to own up to your role in your current status in life.

I don't mean to be harsh, but it's not only time for you to own up to your b.s., it's also time for the next step:

You need to challenge your b.s.!

The ugly truth is sometimes our b.s. is b*llsh*t.

If you haven't caught onto it by now, when I am saying *b.s.* I am referring to your belief system. I have also cross-referenced belief systems to our common colloquial term of b.s. also known as cow dung. The question you should ask yourself is this: "Is my belief system a bunch of b.s.?" This vulgar slang term is defined as "stupid or untrue talk or writing." Another definition of b*llsh*t is "exaggerated lying; to attempt to persuade someone to believe something that isn't true."

Many of us have told someone, "Hey, quit b.s.ing me" or "Don't b.s. me," when dealing with someone trying to pull one over on us.

There's even a card game based on this concept of calling people out on their lies.

In the card game "B.S." there's one object: get rid of all of your cards by any means necessary. There are many variations and styles of play, but essentially, a player lays down 1-4 cards at a time by announcing out loud to the other players what card they played. For example, if it were my turn and I didn't have any eights, and the selected card to play was eight, I could put down a three and say, "One eight." My turn would be over and now it's the next player's turn. If someone suspected that I was lying, they must shout "B.S.!!!" before the next player goes. If nothing is said, one cannot come back later and retroactively call their bluff.

Life is a lot like the "B.S." card game.

Every day in life we are bombarded by a bunch of b.s. In this case, I mean both belief systems and just plain ole b.s. Everyone is offering what they claim to be "truth" and will stop at nothing to get you to accept it as your own. People have their own ambitions and hidden agendas and will stop at nothing to accomplish them by "any means necessary." Although life is similar to the card game, there is one huge difference that makes life much easier.

Unlike the game, your turn isn't over until you take your last breath. If you're reading this it's too late to give up, but it's not too late to keep going. You can always call b.s.

on those people who put that label on you as a child. You can call b.s. on that teacher who told you that you wouldn't amount to anything. You can call b.s. on that relative who judged your teenage pregnancy. You have the liberty to stop being the victim in your situation and start being the victor. This reminds me of one of my favorite songs entitled, *Let Your Power Fall* by James Fortune and FIYA. The lyrics say,

"Let your power fall

When your name is called

Prove the doubters wrong

You're still mighty and strong."

I bet, just like me your favorite lyric in that song would be the "prove the doubters wrong." We love to feed off that energy of "having a chip on our shoulder." Any song, speech or sermon that references "haterz" always gets a good response. We don't realize that there will never be enough evidence for the man that has something to prove. If you accomplish something just to prove someone else wrong, when you finally do reach the pinnacle of your success, you will realize that your victory is shallow and empty.

The emptiness is created by the void that exists because now there's no one to prove wrong. You can either deal with it or find a new enemy or hater to fuel you. If you find yourself entangled in this vicious cycle, you'll be distracted from your real enemy:

Yourself.

I don't know about you, but I'm usually my own harshest critic. There is nothing you can say about me that I haven't said or thought about myself to a harsher degree. Psychology has taught me that the voice in our head that directs our self-talk is developed in our formative years and is a combination of our experiences, how our parents and other authority figures spoke to us, and the behavior they

Challenge the B.S.

modeled. While this is very true, we are not here to throw pity parties, point the finger or avoid taking ownership of the course of our lives. The notion of fault versus responsibility is always at work.

What they did to you is not your fault...

...but how you respond to what happened to you is YOUR responsibility.

Many of us have allowed other people's b.s. to shape our belief systems. We have allowed their insecurities, labels, opinions, and thoughts about who they *think* we are to impact what *we* believe about ourselves. Yes, people may have said terrible things to you, believed negative things about you, and committed ugly acts against you, but we should never allow other people's problems to become our own. Easier said than done. Trust me, I know!

Many of us are not where we want to be in life, but it's not due to a lack of effort. We often put forth a ton of effort but have not understood that most of the time it's wasted because it isn't directed toward the right place. For example, growing up—for whatever reason—my mom would ask me to take the meat for dinner out of the freezer before she left for work. On several occasions, I would forget. I honestly don't remember a time when she asked me to take it out and I actually remembered to do it. Of course, when she would come back home and realize I had not done what she asked, I would try to show her any other positive thing I had done that day. "But Mom, look how clean my room is." "I know I forgot to take out the chicken, but I got a good grade on my test today." Those things are nice, but to her it didn't matter because the one thing she asked me to do, I didn't do.

We are out of order because we are out of order.

There are two contexts in which the phrase "out of order" can be used. One means out of commission or not functioning properly, and the other means not in the correct sequence. Life is not just about doing the right things and making the right choices. It's just as important to do the right things as it is to do the right thing at the right time. Many of us fail to truly evolve because

> we attempt to change our behaviors before we change our beliefs.

Just as we learned from the people who built the Millennium Tower, if you build something on a bad foundation, you're going to pay the price later.

I learned this lesson from the movie *Facing the Giants*. In the movie, a soccer player was making the transition to football as a placekicker and struggled early on. In one of the scenes he missed a kick at the end of a game and began to lose confidence. He told his father, "I knew I was gonna miss it before I even kicked it." His father looked at him and said, "Your actions will always follow your beliefs." Even though that movie came out over thirteen years ago, I have never forgotten that quote.

Just as the title suggests, we all face giants in our lives. It doesn't matter what area of life is your "giant," the key to victory for all of us is the same: correcting our mindset. Our actions are just by-products of how we think.

> Remember, your actions will ALWAYS follow your beliefs.

I believe that whatever we meditate on the most, we manifest. Some people refer to it as the law of attraction. Others may call it a self-fulfilling prophecy, but I have noticed that expectations are magnetic. Common wisdom says that the key to changing our beliefs is to alter our thoughts, but that is a big mistake. Like I stated earlier, you cannot think negative thoughts and expect positive results. Attempting

Challenge the B.S.

to fight thoughts with thoughts is like trying to put out a fire with fire. Transforming your belief system is a culmination of multiple things.

As an operating system is to a smartphone, so are your beliefs to you. The software on any electronic device is what controls everything it is capable of doing. If you have a phone that hasn't updated its software for an extended period of time, it will begin to malfunction. For most of us, our core beliefs were shaped during our formative years. By the age of seven or eight years old we have been given our belief system. Many of us are discouraged because we have been operating on this same level of thinking since that age and wonder why our life isn't the way we want it to be. It's time for a change.

I believe there are four things that need to happen in order to transform our mindsets by challenging our belief system. In the words of Frederick Douglass, "Without struggle, there is no progress." You didn't get to the place where you are in life overnight so you can't expect to fix everything in one day. But, if you are willing to practice patience and focus on the process and not on the outcome, you will eventually end up where you are trying to be.

The first part of the process is rejection. You cannot trust everything you think. I want you to reject everything negative. Reject every temptation to speak or think negatively about yourself. Negativity is not always the absence of truth. There are certain things that **really** happen to you that are negative. There may be things that you do not like about yourself. You may be in a place in life where you feel "stuck." You can acknowledge the truth and realities of life without having a negative perspective about them or having a victim's mentality.

Rejecting negativity alone is not enough. I'm not sure if you're anything like me, but I have a bad habit—that I'm working through—of filling in the unknown with something negative. All throughout the day you are having an on-going conversation with yourself. Rejecting is the process of unlearning all of the patterns of negative self-talk that you have conditioned yourself to do repeatedly. The next step is to begin to replace those negative thought patterns and pessimistic self-talk with words of affirmation and hope.

"Don't let YOU talk to YOU like that!"

I believe we all value being respected. It is something I believe is a universal concept across cultures, countries, and continents. What stuns me the most is how much of a double standard we have when it comes to giving respect. Some of us are quick to say, "Man, if I were you, I wouldn't let them talk to me like that!" but then we turn around and demean ourselves with our own poor self-talk.

You cannot demand others to respect you if you don't have self-respect first.

The key to changing your external world is always to start within. The Bible says, "Love your neighbor as yourself" (Mark 12:31 NLT). Many people misconstrue this and think it is promoting selfishness, but it is not. Whether we consciously intend to or not, we naturally love others in the same way that we love ourselves. We speak to people in a manner that parallels our own self-talk (maybe a little diluted because we're concerned with our image and reputation, of course). On the flip side, people sense our level of self-esteem and self-respect and return to us what we say is acceptable. The reason most people are baffled as to why people interact with them the way they do is because of a lack of self-reflection on their part. Remember, your actions will always follow your beliefs, and your self-respect is the gauge people will use to determine their level of respect for you. No matter where you are on this journey, it's never too late for change, my friend.

As you are simultaneously rejecting negativity and re-placing it with truth and words of affirmation, you will begin to reprogram your mind. Your brain is composed of neural pathways that send signals that direct everything you do. It takes between four weeks and 90 days to form a new neural pathway in the brain. Rome wasn't built in a day. This reminds me of a conversation during my adolescence with my NaNa (I pronounce it *Nay-Nuh* for all the *Nah-nuh* people out there). I was telling her that I had struggled with my self-confidence for years, so it was probably going to take years for me to overcome my lack of self-belief. She looked at me and said something so simple yet so profound:

"It doesn't have to."

I know that doesn't seem like much of a statement, but I believe a new neural pathway was created in my brain during that conversation. I had just assumed that because I struggled with something for years, it would literally take the same amount of years to find freedom from it. But in the words of that sage of a woman, my NaNa: "It doesn't have to."

"But D'Andre, you don't get it, man.
I've tried to stop gambling for years."

"D, I have had this eating disorder since I was a teen."

"Dre, that sounds all good and stuff, but I got a record.
There's no hope for me."

Because I love you and I care for you, I must lovingly tell you something real quick (yea, I know it's supposed to be "really quickly," but I digress)

S H U T U P ! ! !

Your words are powerful! The Bible says, "Death and life are in the power of the tongue and those who love it will eat its fruits." (Proverbs 18:21 ESV)

What kind of diet are you on?

Out of the Ashes

Are you on a *negatarian* diet? (I just made that up)

Do you speak death, destruction and despair over your life?

You are what you eat, and all of those hopeless remarks are not going to digest well. Does that mean just thinking positive and speaking positive will magically make all of your worries and problems disappear? No! But, wallowing in a pit of self-pity and feeling sorry for yourself definitely won't change anything and it will also be a hindrance to your progress.

I'm not pushing a gimmick. Speaking life still requires embracing the reality of your situation while expecting a better future. As I stated earlier, "We acknowledge the harsh realities of life while still hoping for improbable possibilities." The reality is that your situation is not going to change overnight. But just because it won't change overnight, that doesn't mean it has to take forever. You are exactly where you are in life because of what you believe, so if you want your life to change, it's time to start with yourself.

"How you gonna win, when you ain't right within?"- "

That Thing" by Lauryn Hill

You are "more than a conqueror! It's time to turn all of your losses into lessons and win in this next season of your life. But the change you are seeking in your external world starts between your ears and flows from there. But I have a question for you:

Are you ALL IN?!

While you ponder your answer, let's review the process.

Step 1: Reject ALL negativity and falsehood.

Step 2: Replace negativity with positivity, affirmation, and truth.

Step 3: Commit to doing the first two for 90 days **consistently.**

Step 4: ?

The final part of this process is what everyone wants, but not everyone is willing to pay the price.

Renewal.

We all have parts of ourselves whether it be physically, psychologically or emotionally that we want to be made new. The change you need to make in your life is simple, but it is only as easy as you make it. The Bible says, "Do not be conformed to the ways of this world, but **be transformed by the renewal of your mind**..." (Romans 12:2 ESV). The renewal is not a finite destination, but an on-going process. Day by day you must repeat steps 1 through 3 to continue to manifest the renewal and transformation from your old way of living and thinking into your new enlightened and empowered self. Consistency is key. Many times we fail to realize our potential because we lack the patience to see the process all the way through to the end.

TINSTAFL:

There is no such thing as a free lunch.

We must realize that the best things in life aren't free. Sure, some of the greatest things life has to offer don't have a monetary price tag, but there is always a price. What you choose to buy is up to you.

> Indecision is still a decision.

Whether you choose to take ownership of your life or not, both decisions come with a cost. Behind door #1 is a life full of regret and "shoulda, coulda, wouldas." When you embrace a victim mentality, you blame others for all of your problems and render yourself hopeless and utterly helpless to change your situation.

> Blame is a conductor of responsibility.

Out of the Ashes

The power to change any situation lies in the hands of the one who is willing to take the responsibility. No matter how great the pain the "theys" of your life may have inflicted upon you, you are the one who has to live with how you respond. But I know that deep down inside is an overcomer who is waiting to be released from the chains of doubt and fear so that you can become who you were destined to be. There is another option for you if you so choose.

Behind door #2 is a life full of joy, hope, wonder, and fulfillment. These and choicer blessings are bestowed upon the person who takes responsibility for their life and doesn't allow the fate of their future to be in the clutches of those who have hurt them in the past. This person does not subscribe to limiting beliefs but seeks to foster a growth mindset in everything they seek to accomplish. A man or woman of this fortitude knows there are always reasons not to do something, but always believes the reasons to go forward far outweigh the reasons to quit.

"Whatever you are not changing, you are choosing."

Many of us continue down a path of unhealthy behaviors, remain in abusive relationships, tolerate bad business partnerships, and a myriad of other things that are not in our best interests because comfort is our number one value in our lives. (More on values in the final chapter.) It's kind of sick when you think about it.

If you aren't where you know you should be in life—in any given area—it's because you value comfort above all other things.

This is so troubling to me because there are millions of people all across the world who are disgusted by the situations they are in, but they stay simply out of familiarity

Challenge the B.S.

and the fear of the unknown. When you begin to venture down the path of self-discovery and purpose, the unknown actually becomes attractive. What makes it so enticing is that it empowers you to be the author of your own story. Shame and guilt harness the pain of your past to keep you from realizing your potential, but when you live a life of purpose in the present and anticipate the future with hopeful expectation, you immobilize shame and guilt. This can only happen when you value growth over comfort. In other words:

"Get comfortable being uncomfortable."

Wanna know something that's really uncomfortable?

The truth.

Taking ownership requires the courage and willingness to be honest with yourself. Remember, the change you're seeking starts within and anything that is going to have significant substance and longevity must be built on a foundation of truth.

Earlier, I spoke of my battle with pornography and the effect it was having on my life. I was caught in a cycle of sin, guilt, and shame. I would have seasons of victory and then, eventually, a relapse. I was trying to modify my behavior without changing my beliefs—to no avail. There comes a point in everyone's life when feeling bad about something is no longer enough. Saying, "Well, I tried," (*MJ Shrug) can no longer be acceptable. Yes, it was true that I was exposed to porn at a young age. Yes, my innocence was taken from me in the blink of an eye. But, if I am being fair, I also made some poor choices later in life that put me on a path for it to become a major problem for me. I had to stop hiding behind the excuses, the pain, the guilt, and the shame and accept full responsibility for the change I was seeking. Taking ownership means taking action!

After years of battling this alone, I had to realize I needed support. I had a dream of overcoming this battle with pornography and experiencing victory. I wanted to be able to share my story with others and help people to not make the same mistakes I had made, or at the very least, not make them for as long as I did. I invited some friends into my life to hold me accountable and even purchased software that sends them weekly reports for an added layer of accountability. My desire to be the person I knew I was capable of becoming eclipsed my need for comfort.

How bad do you want it?

What is "it" for you?

"It" could be a financial goal.

"It" could be a career-related ambition.

"It" could simply be improving relationships with the ones you love.

Just know that change doesn't come easy. Your commitment to your goal is going to be challenged, and if your "why" isn't big enough, then you'll fold under the pressure. On the contrary, when your reason for change is bigger than yourself, you will have the passion to endure any and every obstacle that comes your way.

Don't put off till tomorrow what can be done today. Take ownership and take charge of the direction of your life.

Say, There are a lot of things that happened in my life that were not my fault, but any change I want to see in my life is my responsibility.

Chapter 9

LIVE IN YOUR PURPOSE

> "Until you find your purpose in life, it's your purpose to find it."

Finding your purpose takes a lot of self-work. It has always been there, but there's usually a lot of stuff getting in the way of you realizing its presence in your life. That is why this is the last chapter. The Bible is filled with promises from God, but each promise requires you to endure a process of applying a principle before it can be manifested in your life. It reminds me of a moth and its cocoon.

A moth is the actual insect that forms a cocoon while a butterfly forms a chrysalis. Both insects, the moth and butterfly, are referred to as pupas before making it to their final stage. The butterfly pupa forms its chrysalis by hardening its own outer layer, while a moth forms a protective casing by spinning silk to create the structure it will use to protect itself. There is a nugget of wisdom that these two creatures have to offer us:

You can allow pain to harden you and make you bitter, or you can repurpose it for your benefit.

The calamities of life will either make you bitter or better. Are you the butterfly? Have you allowed life's calamities to form a callous outer shell around your heart? Many men like me use indifference as a shield against disappointment. "If I don't care, they can't hurt me!" we say to ourselves. Behind that false bravado of the man is a wounded boy in search of healing. I had to learn this summer that the adult D'Andre can be fine. He can achieve and perform at will, but D'Andre the boy still lives inside of the man and he still needs healing. I made the decision to go down the path of the moth.

The moth doesn't harden itself. Rather, it spins its cocoon from the silk it secretes. There are many variations of the word *spin*. One meaning of spin is to put your own ingenious twist onto something. You often hear it in the culinary industry when someone says something like, "He took that pasta dish and put a creole spin on it."

How are you gonna "spin" the pain, disappointment and challenges in your life?

What creative, ingenious twist are you gonna put on all of what you've been through?

Finally, once the moth has formed its cocoon, it molts one last time before its final stage. Molting is when an animal sheds old feathers, hair, skin, or an old shell to make room for new growth. With the wrong perspective, this process may seem unbearable. The moth is surrounded, seemingly trapped, alone and its sight is limited to its current environment.

Can you relate?

Has life caused you to feel surrounded, trapped and alone?

Have you been in a place in which you couldn't see past your current situation?

I have great news for you: this is exactly the type of conditions needed for your transformation. However, it's time for you to "molt" one last time. There are some things that you need to shed yourself of in your life.

What is it for you?

Releasing the lie that your life is an accident?

Removing the labels people placed on you?

Letting go of anxiety?

Finding freedom from addiction?

Whatever it is for you, I am here to tell you that you are knocking at the door of your destiny, but in order to walk through that door, you must let go of the dead weight of disappointment. No longer can the fear of failure guide your decision-making. It's time to unshackle yourself from the chains of anxiety and addiction and walk in the liberating freedom of living in your purpose.

Storytime is over, now it's time to get practical.

I want you to think of what you really value in life.

Simple question, right?

If you're anything like me, at first this may be a difficult question to answer. If you've allowed others to label you, addiction to control you, fear to lead you, or shame to hinder you in life, you may have no clue as to what your true values are.

If you aren't sure, there is one simple way to determine what you value. Ask yourself this question:

Where do I spend the majority of my **time** and **money**?

Live in Your Purpose

The Bible says, "Wherever your treasure is, there the desires of your heart will also be" (Matthew 6:21 ESV). Money is very important, and it does have value, but our time is even more precious because there is no way to get it back once it's gone. How you spend your time is the most important indicator of whether or not you're going to be able to live in your purpose.

For many of us, the perplexing part about this is how we spend our time and money is not necessarily a true reflection of what we value. Often, our time and money can be indicators of our vices instead of our true core values. We discussed addiction, anxiety, identity issues, and acknowledged that everyone has some sort of pain that they have experienced in life. Although we all have different ways of coping with the pain, these are often rooted in the same thing—escapism.

Don't live a life you have to escape, build a life that you cannot wait to wake up in the morning and experience."
-@DJLinspires

I missed so much of my life trying to escape it!

I'd be at work looking forward to getting off. It would be Monday and I would already be thinking about Friday. I was always looking forward to the next social event that I would be attending or my next vacation. The irony is that when I finally left work, made it to Friday, went to the event or was on vacation, it was usually underwhelming and disappointing. In colloquial terms, "it wasn't worth the hype." I would find myself in the middle of whatever I thought was going to make me feel better and sometimes it would make me feel worse. The weekend never seemed long enough, and then I had to go back to work. The vacation didn't deliver on all my grandiose ideas of what I thought it would be. If you find yourself constantly looking forward to something else just to make it through the day, it's probably time to reevaluate your life.

What I didn't realize at the time was that my life was missing two important components: peace and purpose. These two things go hand in hand. Until I found my purpose, I would never be at peace, and until I had peace, I would never find my purpose. Since peace is a prerequisite to purpose, let's start with that.

> Peace can only be found in the present.

Think about it. Reflect upon a time that you found yourself distressed. One of two things had to be true during that time:

You were dwelling on the past.

You were worried about your future.

The past you that is consuming you could be as far back as your childhood or as current as the person who just cut you off in traffic—but the premise is the same. The future concern that has you worried could be as distant as retirement or as near as the next moment. In both situations, we are not allowing ourselves to be fully present and engaged in the current moment. As we discussed in Chapter 8, in order for renewal to take place, we must replace our negative habits with behaviors that benefit us.

"Purpose Over Pleasure"- Jonathan Traylor

The turning point for me was when I chose to give up my addictions, insecurities, and excuses in exchange for becoming the man God created me to be. I realized that the temporary moments of pleasure or distraction they brought me were not worth the greater purpose God had for my life.

So what do you really value?

Respect?

Honesty?

Faith?

Time?

Creativity?

Once you are able to articulate your values, it's time for some more self-reflection. It's time for a moment of truth. You must decide how important your purpose is to you. TINSTAFL, remember? It's going to cost you something.

Any people, situations, or temptations that cause you to violate your values gotta go! Not everyone can go where you are headed. It's not even so much that you need to call people and "cut them off," because as you begin staying true to your core values, certain people and situations won't even be attracted to the real you. You won't notice because as you find your authentic self, those same things won't appeal to you anymore either. The good news is that you will also begin to attract new opportunities, people, and resources that will assist you in accomplishing your goals.

Now that you've grounded yourself in peace, it's time to find your purpose. Peace creates the right environment for self-discovery. The stillness and tranquility it offers allows you to think introspectively. Now, it's time to identify your gift.

"Your purpose is the intersection of your gifts and values in order to solve a problem in the world" -@DJLinspires

It's time to identify your gift(s). I truly believe each and every one of us is gifted and talented in some area. I also know we each have more than one gift. But let's just start with one for now.

What is the one thing you can do better than everyone else with minimal effort?

If you're anything like me, this may be a difficult question to answer. Growing up, I always knew I had intellect, but

I didn't consider that a gift. I grew up around people who were gifted athletes, dancers, musicians, and singers, and I always felt out of place and forgotten. In one of his sermons,

> TD Jakes once said that we are the last ones to identify our gift. He said we normalize our exceptionality because we live with it on a daily basis.

If you're not careful, this is how you can position yourself to be used and taken advantage of by people. When people notice that you don't value yourself or are not aware of how precious your gift is, they will harness it for their own benefit without giving you anything in return.

Looking back on my life, I now realize that I have been gifted. The reason I felt as though I wasn't is because I didn't have a platform or outlet to express my gifts. As a child and adolescent I enjoyed writing poetry, writing stories, drawing, and speaking. I participated in this after-school program through the YMCA called Youth & Government and represented my city at the state level in it three times. I just didn't view my creative writing and speaking as *real gifts* and I didn't have consistent outlets to express my talents and affirm myself. As a teenager, I finally began to get a glimpse of how gifted I was.

Like many other people, I first discovered my gift in church. After moving to Houston with my uncle as a teenager, I was afforded the opportunity to spend more time with some of my cousins. One of those cousins, Michael, (who is more like an older brother to me) was a part of a rap group with a few other teenage boys who performed at churches and church events all across Houston. I was attending one of their performances and right before they were about to go up, Michael asked me to join them. I profusely refused. I was shy, timid and suffering from anxiety at the time. There

Live in Your Purpose

was no way I was going to get on that stage! One of my other cousins pestered me with peer pressure and everyone convinced me to go. As they were introducing us, I was so nervous, and I did not feel like I belonged up there with them. Then the unthinkable happened: there was a technical problem with the music! As we stood there awkwardly waiting on the audio/visual team to fix the problem, something even crazier happened: I picked up a microphone and started to speak.

Our song was called "S.O.C." (Soldiers of Christ) and there is no way I could possibly describe in writing how fire that song was, but it was fire! I said something along the lines of "if you are a soldier for Christ, let me hear you make some noise" or something like that. I began to pump up the crowd and fill the dead space long enough for everyone to resolve the problem. I eventually joined the group, performed with them at events, and even wrote some verses on several songs. At one point, I was really getting serious about the music and thought it might be my path. Unfortunately, like all great groups, we split up, and it was just my cousin and I. Eventually, he moved for a career opportunity and that was the end of that. Now, I was back to square one, feeling like I was talentless. I thank God for the entire experience, because through my now-seasoned, adult eyes, I know that I gained a valuable lesson.

> Never confuse your actual gift with an expression of your gift.

Many of us miss out on our purpose in life because we put ourselves in a box. We have an encounter with one medium in which we can demonstrate our talent and convince ourselves it is the only way we can do so. When I was younger, I was set on becoming a lawyer. At the time, it was the only way I felt I could monetize what I deemed were my strengths: writing, critical thinking, and speaking.

Then, I encountered music, and also thought that was my path because it felt so natural to be on stage in front of others and using that platform to share my faith. What I came to realize is some of my gifts were wisdom, exhortation, speaking, and creativity. I could use all of these gifts as a songwriter, television personality, lawyer, or even an author. Rapping wasn't my gift. The gift was the ability to inspire people, to speak and to use God's word to do so. Rapping was just one way of me doing that. Drawing and writing poetry weren't my gifts, while creativity was. Those just happened to be the first few ways of expressing it that I had encountered.

So, what is YOUR gift?

Once you've identified your gift, it's time to find a problem?

Yes, go look for a problem.

What do you hate?!

What in this world, ignites passion in you at just the very thought of it?

You are what you hate!

Show me what you hate, and it'll show me what you aren't willing to tolerate. If you aren't willing to tolerate it, you will go to extreme lengths to resolve or eradicate the issue. This is your passion which is connected to your purpose.

For example, I hate walking in a room and seeing people suffer from anxiety because I once struggled with it myself. I hate seeing people make decisions in life based on fear, because I once made EVERY decision in my life based on fear. I hate it when I see talented people who don't see it in themselves because it took me the longest time to truly believe I was a person of value. But there is one thing I hate the most! I could go on and one about things I hate, but this sums them all up:

Live in Your Purpose

> I hate seeing people live beneath their purpose!

When someone else does something that irritates us, it's usually because we see a reflection of ourselves in them. A coworker of mine, Timothy J. Nelson, author of *Jesus Peace,* once said something that really stuck with me, and I'll never forget it! He came to my church to promote his book *What If You're Wrong About You* and in speaking he said this:

"Many people compliment me for being humble, but really my humility is a lack of confidence in myself."

What he said resonated with me tremendously. I saw so much of myself in what he shared. It was so easy for me to identify the greatness in others, give them all of this advice on what they should do to tap into it, but not have enough belief in myself to take my own advice. After spending my life lacking confidence in my own abilities, in the spring of 2018, I finally took action and began the journey of walking in my purpose.

My goal was to put the purpose of my life into one sentence. I knew that if I could do this, it would give me a singular focus. Having a clear idea of who I was would be fundamental in creating the life that God had called me to live. I know what you're probably thinking, "How can I take my life and sum it up in just one sentence?" I once thought the same thing, until I realized it could fit into a few easy steps.

Determine 5-6 core values you want to live your life by.

Identify your gifts and talents.

Find a problem you want to solve in the world.

Find a way you can use your gifts to solve the problem without violating your values.

After going through the process of putting my existence into one sentence, I came to this realization: there was purpose in my pain! My pain was not a punishment, but it was positioning me for my God-ordained assignment.

> The adversity I endured was merely a compass pointing me toward my destiny.

The scars I carried with me were not just signs of my suffering—they were evidence of my survival!

I had survived all of my worst days!

My name is D'Andre Jamal Lacy. I was born in the rural, small town known as Palestine, Texas to two young parents who weren't expecting my arrival. I've battled anxiety, depression, low self-esteem, and even wrestled with the desire to live. I used to pray to God to "just let me stay asleep." I've had an addiction to pornography and masturbation. I've self-medicated with food to find comfort. I've lost countless hours of sleep to post-traumatic stress disorder. I nearly flunked out of college. I've been underemployed, unemployed, and I have had negative bank account balances. I've been called all sorts of things besides my name. I used to think my life didn't matter.

Then, I fully surrendered my life to Jesus Christ and accepted Him as my savior. But things didn't instantly improve. I struggled even after receiving salvation, but at every turn I was met by His unfailing love. His love began to transform my heart. I let go of my sins, fears, doubts, and worries so I could grab hold of His grace, promises, and forgiveness. In Him, I found my true identity and purpose.

In the words of Sean Carter aka Jay-Z, "Allow me to re-introduce myself!"

If you knew me ten years ago, then you don't know me anymore.

My name is D'Andre Jamal Lacy. My personal vision is to inspire people to discover their God-given purpose. My

Live in Your Purpose

mission is to share wisdom in various forms of media to educate and empower people. This book is my first, but it will not be my last. I will spend the rest of my life working to manifest this vision from God while giving Him all of the glory for any success that comes as a result.

And I have some great news for you:

If God can do it for someone, as messed up as I was (and still am), He can do it for you, too!

The time for excuses has ended. The time for waiting is over. Destiny awaits you!

If you're willing to do the work, have the patience to endure the process, and possess the audacity to find hope in the face of hopeless situations, then buried beneath all of the wounds, scars, and pains of your past is your purpose in life.

Say this aloud to yourself, "God has gifted me to solve a problem and to be a problem! I am fearfully and wonderfully made, and the time is now for me to discover my purpose!"

Now, it's time to walk in it!

CONCLUSION

I want to be a tree when I grow up!

Yes, you read that right, I said, "I want to be a tree when I grow up!" But, not just any tree, I want to be a Sequoia!

But why the Sequoia?

There are three reasons why I want to embody the traits of this tree:

The first reason is its stature. Sequoias can grow to be 30 feet in diameter and more than 250 feet tall. The grandest of them all resides in Sequoia National Park and stands at 275 feet tall, has a 102-foot diameter and weighs over 2 million pounds. This is not the only admirable trait of this majestic tree.

The second reason I am fond of the Sequoia tree is due to its lifespan. The sequoia tree can live up to 3,000 years. The longest recorded Sequoia lived for more than 3,500 years. But the final reason may be the most inspiring.

Sequoias need fire to survive!

The heat of forest fires aids the sequoia tree in many ways. The seeds of the tree are housed near its base within small, green cones. Unless a fire or insect forces the cone to crack open, the seeds can remain dormant for up to twenty years! Fire forces the cones to crack open and release their seed into the soil for future development. In addition, sometimes forest fires aid in clearing dead trees and other vegetation to create room for something new to grow.

This life cycle is reminiscent of another creature I am fond of, the phoenix.

In Part I: The Fire, we learned that just like the phoenix and sequoia we all must go through a fire. From the time we entered the world, we have, at some point wrestled with our existence. Before we can walk in our purpose, we must understand that we are not an accident. No matter what conditions we were conceived in or what type of environment we were born into, believing we are not an accident allows us to embrace our origins. Once we embrace our origins, we can remove the labels that people, our past, and our pain have placed upon us because we understand our true identity.

At the end of every fire is a pile of ashes.

In Part II: The Ashes, we discussed what's left behind after the fire. Many of us are left feeling hopeless but holding onto our hope is necessary. We can have everything, but without hope, we really have nothing. We can have nothing, but with hope, we have everything. Even while remaining hopeful, there may be things in our past that we must mourn. The natural tendency is just to bury our pain, but we learned that to truly move forward, we don't bury our pain to hide it. Rather, we hold a funeral service for it to lay it to rest. Our innocence is something we all lose and must all come to grips with in order to be made whole. Part of pursuing wholeness is addressing the addictions we have developed in life as a way of coping with our pain. I led by example by confessing my own battle with pornography, masturbation, and using food to cope with the challenges of life. I urge you to do the same by identifying, addressing, and finding accountability to overcome whatever you may be using to self-medicate.

Although it seems hopeless, out of the pile of ashes, a majestic phoenix rises to begin its life anew!

In Part III: The Rebirth, we discovered that there is hope for all of us when we are willing to do the self-work to become the best versions of ourselves. This self-work begins with taking ownership of our lives. Although we have all faced trauma, experienced pain, and had to live in many circumstances out of our control, there are more things in our control than we realize. Once we take ownership, we are empowered to challenge the b.s. in our lives—faulty belief systems. Our actions always follow our beliefs so we cannot hope to ever change our behavior or our lives without changing our belief systems first. The final step of our rebirth is living in our purpose.

You were created to utilize your gifts while living in your values in order to solve a problem in the world. Once you are able to articulate your values and identify your gifts, then you will be able to craft a personal vision statement and mission statement for your life.

We all work for or lead organizations that have clearly defined roles, rules regulations, and expectations of their employees. Every successful organization has mission and vision statements in order to ensure that their purpose is fulfilled. I challenge you to articulate your values, identify your gifts, and put the purpose of your life into one sentence. This one sentence will give you a singular focus which will allow you to make decisions that support the life you are seeking to build.

You were born on purpose and for a purpose.

Now it's time for you to take the necessary steps to walk in it!

Thank you!

I am appreciative of your support by purchasing this book. My hope is that you are inspired to take action towards your purpose. I want as many people as possible to be blessed by the contents of this book, so I have a few favors to ask to ensure that this message touches as many lives as possible:

1. Leave an honest review on the platform you purchased the book.
2. Follow me on all the social media platforms listed on this page.
3. Take a picture with the book and post your thoughts with the hashtag #DJLinspires. Make sure you tag me in it, so I can share your post.

My name is D'Andre Jamal Lacy and my purpose in life is to educate, inspire and empower people to live in their purpose. There is at least one thing that you do better than everyone else in this world with less effort. I pray you discover your gift, use your pain as a compass to point you in the direction of a problem you'd like to solve in the world, and use your gift to be a solution without violating your values.

Instagram:@DJLinspires

Twitter: @DJLinspires

Facebook: www.Facebook.com/DJLinspires

Website: www.DJLinspires.com

Made in the USA
Coppell, TX
14 March 2022

74951809R00077